ROB FROST

ROB FROST

Reflections on a Life Well Lived

Compiled by Andy Frost with assistance from
David Somers

Authentic

MILTON KEYNES ● COLORADO SPRINGS
● HYDERABAD

First published 2008 by Authentic Media
9 Holdom Avenue, Bletchley, Milton Keynes, Bucks, MK1 1QR, UK
1820 Jet Stream Drive, Colorado Springs, CO 80921, USA
OM Authentic Media, Medchal Road, Jeedimetla Village,
Secunderabad 500 055, A.P., India
www.authenticmedia.co.uk

Authentic Media is a division of IBS-STL U.K., limited by guarantee, with
its Registered Office at Kingstown Broadway, Carlisle, Cumbria CA3 0HA.
Registered in England & Wales No. 1216232. Registered charity 270162

British Library Cataloguing in Publication Data
A catalogue record for this book is available from the
British Library

ISBN-13: 978-1-85078-804-1

Cover Design by David Lund
Print Management by Adare
Printed and bound by J.H. Haynes & Co., Sparkford

Contents

Introduction

Andy Frost

It was an ordinary day in the office – the regular mix of vision, discussion, creativity and banter. And then in a moment everything changed . . . with one phone call.

'Rob, it's for you.'

I knew it was serious. His face focused and the tone in his voice became eerily surprised. He gripped the phone tightly. 'Yes, I understand . . . thanks,' he said. Then he firmly placed the phone back on its cradle and turned to face me. 'The tests have come back positive. It is cancer.'

The office suddenly became silent as Rob regurgitated the full contents of the phone call. The very word 'cancer' seemed to infect the bubbling atmosphere like a poisoned dart.

We knew cancer. It had only been a year earlier that we had lost Camille from the office team to cancer. She was an always-smiling 34-year-old Kiwi who injected enthusiasm and grace into every encounter.

As he spoke, a flurry of questions beavered their way through my mind. A sense of disbelief. A sense of uncertainty. A sense of impossibility. I felt like crying.

Moments later, after prayer with the office team, Dad and I walked round to the nearby coffee shop to unpack what was happening. We sat opposite each other, sipping coffee between our prolonged silences.

Rob's emotions seemed to be swinging like a pendulum. The silence was punctuated with, 'Well, I have had a good life . . . I don't have any regrets.' I could see in his eyes that he was beginning to stare death in the face. And then, as the emotional pendulum swung the other way, he rebuked himself with a hopeful, 'It will probably all be okay.'

That was the start of this journey . . . a journey full of ups and downs . . . of precious moments . . . of desperate prayers . . . a journey that came to a climax less than five months later in a hospital intensive care unit.

The cancer had spread all over his liver and spleen in a matter of weeks. He passed into unconsciousness, and one by one the medical machines were withdrawn from his bedside.

His stomach continued to swell and contract with every breath, and his whitened face looked tired and worn . . . and then he was gone. Off into eternity. In that last moment his eyes opened wide one last time. No more breath.

My Mum, my brother Chris and a few close friends were gathered around, and a mixture of tears and hugs filled the room as we prayed one last time that God would take him into eternity. His earthly journey had come to an end. It was a holy moment.

For the last few days of his life, we had sat around hospital wards. When death became the inevitable outcome, there came the time to say goodbye. This was probably the hardest thing that I have ever done. How do you try to say what needs to be said? The gist of what I said to him was 'Thank you.' Thank you for being a role model for me throughout my life. This book is an opportunity for us to thank God for a good life and say our goodbyes.

During my teenage years, I had never wanted to work with my Dad. Amidst my rebellious teenage angst there had been lots of conflict. I had felt that he just didn't understand me. But then my return to faith and my time away at University began to heal the wounds from those difficult days. And at the age of 21 I agreed to work with my Dad. It had never been part of my plan, but God seemed to be instigating it.

And so for the last seven years of my life, my Dad has been not just a father but also a mentor, a work colleague, a friend and a house-mate. These years have drawn us closer together and set me on a path that I never expected.

It has been an adventure – dreaming, scheming, planning and creating. And as the adventure goes on, I know that I will continue to miss him. As I see some of his vision become reality, I am saddened that he is not a part of it.

There are still some days when, as I wake, I think his death has all been a nightmare. But in the cold light of day, I know that he has stepped into eternity to be with his Maker.

I don't believe that death was ever part of God's perfect plan, but in this world our mortality is a concept that we can't escape. When we are faced with issues of mortality, everything is put into perspective. What will our brief time on planet earth have counted for?

Rob made Jesus Lord of his life and accomplished great things for the Kingdom. When I try to explain what my Dad did, it's hard to box him into one mould. He had a multitude of God-given gifts and he could be described in so many ways . . . as a visionary, a media guru, a preacher, a mobilizer or, for me, a Dad. However people saw him, the one thing that is for sure is that Jesus was the driving force that led him to become the man he was.

Though he has now left this world, his legacy lives on in the generation of people who have been mentored, released and empowered through his life. I know that there are many others who would have loved to have contributed to this book, but I hope that these few accounts will paint a picture of a life well lived.

But more than simply remembering a good man, I hope that this book helps us all to put our lives into perspective. I recall those words that my father said: 'I have no regrets.' I hope that as you read the pages of this book, you are challenged to make sure that your life counts. I encourage you, from today, to live full out for Jesus, so that you too will have no regrets.

Here's to a life well lived!

Part 1

Rob Frost in Public

Rob as a Leader

Wes Griffin,
President, International Leadership Institute

When I received the news that Rob Frost was in heaven, I could hardly speak for two days. To imagine this world without him was more than I could easily accept. Rob was many things to many people, including a leader for us all. His influence in my own life was so large that it will take years for me to adjust to a future without him.

Rob and I shared many things. We travelled the world. We preached and taught side by side. We shared late-night conversations and ate strange foods. We told many stories and laughed often. We humbly laid hands on people in prayer and saw God powerfully transform lives. We both battled cancer and claimed the verse of Scripture, 'To live is Christ. To die is gain.' Rob received his reward before me.

Rob never sought to be a leader. His goal was faithfulness to the vision that God had placed in his heart. He understood leadership. He taught leadership. He modelled leadership. But his real goal was the passionate pursuit of God's heart. His leadership was the by-product of that and the price that he was willing to pay for it.

Bringing the Kingdom of God on earth

God's usual way of bringing his Kingdom on earth is to find a person who will serve him with their whole heart. Abraham is called the father of faith. Moses led God's people out of Egypt.

David served with great passion. Esther was born for 'such a time as this'. Each of these persons cooperated with God to lead, inspire, motivate, and eventually leave their mark on human history. God also called out to a man named Rob Frost who said 'yes' to him. History will never be the same.

In 1998, with a small team of other key leaders (including my wife Joy and I), Rob launched an organization called the International Leadership Institute. For the first two years, we conducted global research into the nature of leadership. Three essential characteristics were found in the best leaders, which are illustrated by an equilateral triangle – a symbol of strength and stability. We observed that many leaders possess two of the characteristics, but for different reasons, never fully develop the third side. This insufficiency limits that person's potential and hinders the coming of the Kingdom of God on earth.

Rob Frost was one of those exemplary people who lived out all three characteristics and provided an example for how a Christian should grow and lead in the Body of Christ. The three characteristics are spiritual leadership, servant leadership, and transformational leadership.

Rob as a spiritual leader

Rob was a great leader, someone whom people would naturally follow. One of the open secrets of Rob's great impact as a Christian leader was him clearly being a person who was following Jesus. Throughout his ministry he was involved with hundreds of different missions, conferences, tours and various other projects aimed at furthering the Kingdom of God, but all were inspired by his relationship with God, and by his continual listening to God in order to discern where he should go as a leader. Rob always relied on God rather than himself when it came to leadership.

In the summer of 2006, Rob was the guest speaker for a holiday camp held by a large Californian church. At 4 a.m. one morning, wide awake due to the effects of jet-lag (having flown in from London), he heard God clearly speak to him about a future event to put on. In the quietness of Rob's heart, Jesus said to him, *'Why not organize an event that I would want to come to?'*

The question immediately intrigued Rob, and got his imagination and creativity racing. What would an event that Jesus would want to come to actually look like? Rob recalled, 'I saw the event so clearly that it was as if I was there. It was as if the Body of Christ had woken up after a long sleep and had discovered what fun it was to be alive in God.'

And so the vision for the Pentecost Festival, the largest and most ambitious project Rob ever undertook, was seeded. All of it was birthed out of an intimate relationship with God. The Festival vision has now grown to involve more than 200 local churches and scores of organizations in creating a missional event in multiple venues spread throughout central London. God is the author. Huge numbers of people are involved. Yet, it was Rob's hunger to hear God's voice that launched this new movement.

One of Rob's favourite themes when preaching was 'Leadership and the Power of the Holy Spirit'. On many occasions he told a story of how, as a young Methodist minister stationed in Mitcham, he would take a prayer walk through a local park that passed a small but swiftly flowing stream. One morning the water authorities had siphoned off the flow of water, and all that remained was a slow-moving brown sludge in the river-bed. At that point Rob felt the Holy Spirit say to him, 'That sludge is what the ministry of Rob Frost is like without the anointing and presence of the Spirit.'

Rob never forgot that all worthwhile work of ministry can only be accomplished by the Holy Spirit. First and foremost, Rob remained all his life a spiritual leader and a fellow follower of Jesus Christ.

Rob as a servant leader

The second characteristic of an authentic leader is servant leadership. This concept is familiar today even in secular circles. The foundation of servant leadership is found in Jesus

Christ expressing his love to the disciples by washing their feet. The dominant images in this biblical incident are Christ's hands, a towel, and a basin of water. In one simple act, Jesus provided an example for us to follow:

> And during supper Jesus . . . got up from the table, took off his outer robe, and tied a towel around himself. Then he poured water into a basin and began to wash the disciples' feet and to wipe them with the towel that was tied around him.
>
> Jesus said, 'So if I, your Lord and Teacher, have washed your feet, you also ought to wash one another's feet. For I have set before you an example, that you also should do as I have done to you.'
>
> (Jn. 13:2–5,14–15)

Servant leadership is a simple yet powerful principle. For twenty years Rob was the director of the annual Easter People Christian conference. In 2002 the theme of Easter People was 'Global Vision'. Rob invited key leaders from around the world to help cast a vision for global impact to the ten thousand or more people who attended the event, which took place in three venues. One of the most gracious invitations that Rob ever extended to me was to preach on the Sunday morning at the closing service in the main hall at Torquay. After great consideration, I preached on 'Finishing Well', incorporating a special clip from the movie *Chariots of Fire*. Steph Reese and Anne Salway performed an original skit written for the occasion, and of course, the praise team led an amazing time of inspirational worship.

Several people collaborated on how to conclude the service and bless people before they departed. The decision was to end with an altar invitation for prayer. Rob had attended all three Easter People venues, finishing with us in Torquay. We requested that he be available to pray with people and then give the final benediction. To my surprise and shock, he replied, 'That's not possible; I'll be leaving before the service ends.'

Some would contend that Rob left early due to exhaustion, or his aversion to long goodbyes. I see it differently. Rob left early because he was a servant leader; he did not have to be on stage. He was Easter People's visionary. He was the consummate, master mobilizer. He was the number-one cheerleader. But he did not have to be up front, hearing the crowd's applause, and receiving the adulation of friends. It was enough to have in his hand the towel and the basin. It was enough to simply serve.

The average leader's ego would not allow him or her to walk away at such a moment. Rob was brilliant on the main platform, but his real leadership was always out of the bright lights. His greatest joy was empowering others and seeing them lead. He exemplified servanthood for us all.

Rob as a transformational leader

All true Christian leadership begins with vision: a picture of the future given by God to those with the faith and passion to believe that dreams can become reality. Rob would see the possibilities with both his heart and mind. Then he would invite the rest of us to join him and follow God's call to bring about meaningful change.

Many Christians possess the characteristics of spiritual leadership and servant leadership, but they never develop the third critical characteristic: transformational leadership. Transformation is about meaningful change. It is about seeing a need and then meeting that need. It is not enough to be spiritual by nature and servant oriented. Real leaders change themselves, their followers, and ultimately the world. Transformational leaders are rare and God desperately needs more of them. They see things that others do not see and take actions that others are unwilling to take.

Rob Frost was an agent of change. He would see a need, take up the cause, fully trust God, and move himself and others to action. One example among thousands involved a family from Kosovo.

They were a family of six who had fled from the genocidal wars in the former Yugoslavia to seek asylum in the UK: two parents, two sons, and two daughters. Eventually given a council house in Raynes Park, the family became known to Rob and the local church, and the eldest son became involved with the drama groups and football team. Since their house was just a two-minute walk from Rob's, it was natural that he became a friend to the whole family.

When they had been in Britain for nearly five years, and with a legal application for citizenship being made through the British courts, the police demanded entrance to the house one morning at 4 a.m. They were taken to a nearby airport, and deported back to Kosovo. Given a train ride to a town of their choosing in Kosovo, they were then abandoned with no money, no accommodation, and no support. They were not even allowed to call their solicitor during the deportation, and only managed to contact friends back in the UK when they were in Kosovo.

When Rob heard about what had happened he was incensed by such a flagrant breach of their human rights. He petitioned the local MP, organized a protest march from the local church to their house (which made local and national news bulletins), and even appeared on the Radio 4 *PM* programme to highlight their plight. A solicitor was hired to take up their case, and a firm of barristers was engaged to represent the family in court. It was then that the government finally backed down in the face of such pressure, and after spending just over six months in Kosovo, the family was finally brought home to Raynes Park amid scenes of jubilation.

In all of this whirlwind of activity it was Rob Frost the transformational leader who continually made the plans, mobilized the people, organized the protests, conducted media interviews, and ensured everyone was fixed on the ultimate vision of bringing the family home. He did not rest until they were back, and his ability to threaten the government with court action, and ultimately force them to change policy, is a powerful testimony to his ability as a transformational leader. With Rob on the scene, things did not stay the same! He knew that leadership is about bringing positive change into situations, and he was a master at making this happen.

One hand on his casket – one hand on my heart

During the Hopes and Dream tour, I came from the USA to England to travel with Rob for a couple of days. I needed to be in his presence. I felt that God would speak to me if I was around him. Late one night, long after everyone else had gone to sleep, Rob and I sat talking about the vision that has become the International Leadership Institute (ILI). Sometime around 1 a.m., Rob cocked his head and looked off into the future. With an even tone, he said, 'This is what I see. I see thousands of leaders being trained to follow God's vision for their life and then being mobilized to train others to do the same. I see a movement of people passionately following Christ.' Then, true to form, he laid out several key points and became personally involved to see the vision become reality. Today, ILI's alumni network exceeds 25,000 leaders in 50 nations speaking more than 200 languages. Although an incredibly busy man, Rob gave strategic time to developing ILI's global ministry from the inception of an idea to a growing, global movement. Rob's signature training sessions on 'Leadership and Mobilization' are taught all over the world.

My wife Joy and I took the overnight flight from the USA in order to be at Rob's funeral service. It was a privilege to represent ILI's global family, but I mostly came for me. I needed to say goodbye to my friend, my mentor, and a co-labourer for the harvest. The service at Raynes Park was remarkable both for the sense of loss and the celebration of a great man's life. At the service, Joy and I presented to Jacqui, Andy and Chris a book of tributes from around the world.

After the service at the church, we joined the family and close friends at the crematorium. At the request of the family, the curtain separating the mourners from the casket was not drawn at the conclusion of the service. Instead, one at a time, people began filing past the casket to the exit. Some people paused to pay their final respects.

When my turn came, I found myself standing before the casket, which was situated on a marble slab slightly above eye level. I knew this moment would come, like it does at all funerals. I paused awkwardly and then I did something that I had never before done at a funeral. With one hand I reached out and touched the casket. My other hand went over my heart. A prayer came into my mind: 'Lord, you blessed me to know and love Rob Frost. Now, he is with you in heaven. Let all of us who knew Rob continue his legacy. Fill us with your Spirit, like you did him. Amen.'

Leadership is not an easy task. It is part science and part art. It requires creativity and resolute determination. It involves risks and faith. Leaders blaze new trails.

Rob Frost was a leader. He dreamed God's dreams and led the rest of us into the future that he saw. His life was marked by spiritual passion, a servant's heart, and a deep commitment to transform this world for Christ. Rob set before us an example and he leaves us with a challenge – the challenge to passionately pursue God's heart and fulfil God's greater purposes for our lives.

Rob Frost served as one of the founders of the International Leadership Institute. He led ILI's work in Europe and served as a senior international faculty member, training and mobilizing leaders of leaders around the world.

Contributions have been made to this chapter by Mark Williamson, formerly a staff member at Share Jesus International, and now co-executive director for History Makers, a leadership development initiative birthed with Rob's support through Share Jesus International and the International Leadership Institute.

Rob as an Evangelist

Graham Horsley,
Church Planting Secretary, Methodist Church

My first experience of working with Rob in an evangelistic way was in the summer of 1974. I had met Rob earlier that year when he came to speak at Salford University Methsoc (Methodist Society). A little while later I heard through a friend that he was organizing 'Share Jesus '74' in a group of churches around York. I hitch-hiked to Haxby Methodist Church to join the team and discovered a group of about thirty young people, mostly under twenty. They were led by Rob and two other trainee ministers from Hartley Victoria College. In those days, with no mobile phones or email, it was amazing that Rob could gather such a group from all over the country (though many of them were from Rochdale, where there had been a remarkable move of the Holy Spirit in the previous year). Quite a lot of the team had only been Christians for a few months, most had no experience of evangelism (having been on two Methsoc missions, I was a veteran!), but all of us had a longing for more of God for ourselves and to share what we had found in Jesus with anyone who would listen.

We formed three teams based in local Methodist churches and began a programme of door-to-door visitation, kids' clubs and youth drop-ins that would become the norm for 'Share Jesus' missions in later years. Most of the people we met and shared our faith with were teenagers and children from around the villages. The members of the churches supported the mission, though they were slightly bemused by our youthful enthusiasm! All the team members were called on to give testimony and take part in drama sketches. Those who could played musical instruments, and occasionally Christian rock bands turned up to do concerts – Rob already had an amazing number of contacts. The mission was chaotic in many ways, but the two things that really stick in my memory were the times of prayer and worship that we had as a team and the number of young people who made decisions to become followers of Jesus – many of them at events where Rob preached.

We were a group filled with enthusiasm, but we had very little experience. It was a time of incredible optimism. It was the final phase of the 'hippy era', and many outside the church were looking forward to the 'Age of Aquarius' when, it was believed, peace and love would fill the world. Those of us who were Christians believed that the Holy Spirit would soon renew the church, which would then convert the world. Many of the people who worked with Rob in the early days of his ministry drifted away from the evangelistic fervour that brought us together. Some settled for renewing the church and lost their outward focus; some drifted away from Jesus altogether; some just got tired. In our youthful optimism, we looked at the few 'on fire' older Christians whom we knew – people like Walter Newby and Herbert Silverwood – and hoped that we would stay as fervent as them and not become worn-out or boring – Rob never did! Thirty-three years later, in the last conversation I had with Rob, just ten days before he died, he told me that having cancer simplified things – he now only did things that brought in the Kingdom of God.

Rob had begun his training as an evangelist at Cliff College. From there he offered for the Methodist ministry and was accepted for training at Hartley Victoria College. His passion for evangelism regularly got him into trouble with the college authorities. Ministers in training were expected to be pastors rather than evangelists. It didn't help that he had a wicked sense of humour and carried out pranks on fellow students and staff alike.

In his early years in the ministry, he brought to his preaching and his pastoral care a passion for people to become Christians. All his churches hosted regular missions – the teams were gathered from theological colleges and the large number of young evangelical Christians who were attracted to Rob by his evangelistic leadership skills. As a circuit minister he also took time out to lead teams doing evangelism. Every summer Rob gathered a group together to do evangelism. In 1975 we toured the country in a double-decker bus with the 'Gospel Roadshow' – a mixture of music, drama, testimony and evangelistic preaching. We slept in the bus or on church floors and criss-crossed the country to fit in with local church invitations. A chance meeting at one of the Roadshows with some American tourists led to an invitation to do the Gospel Roadshow USA in 1976, driving from New York to Montreal, performing at churches along the way. In 1977 the Gospel Roadshow went to Lloret de Mar in Spain, where the team stayed at a local campsite and did street-theatre sketches and music in the hotel lounges which were filled with English tourists. Our visit coincided with the first-ever strike in Spain by members of the entertainment union; we only realized later that the hotel owners were happy to have us perform in their lounges as 'scab' labour!

We had a real mix of abilities on the teams. We aimed for excellence in presentation, but enthusiasm and passion for sharing the good news of Jesus gave our performances an edge which they might otherwise have lacked. Rob did most of the preaching, and it was on these tours that he developed a gift for short, powerful evangelistic sermons. This skill was to stand him in good stead when he later had opportunities to 'preach' on secular television.

Although Rob enjoyed local church ministry, it was obvious that his calling was to be an evangelist, and that call was recognized by the whole Methodist Church when Rob was set aside from local ministry to become a full-time evangelist. In the 1980s evangelism was almost a dirty word in the Methodist Church, so this was a courageous move. The whole Church owes a debt to Revd Dr Donald English, the General Secretary of the Home Mission division of the Methodist Church, who made it possible. He not only fought in Rob's corner to get him permission to exercise his ministry, but also offered wise guidance to Rob as his ministry developed.

Rob will perhaps be best remembered as a preaching evangelist. There are many Christians in the church today who made their first commitment at an Easter People celebration or a Share Jesus rally when Rob preached an evangelistic message. His passionate (and often downright loud!) preaching style didn't appeal to everyone, but he adapted well to varying audiences and saw hundreds of people respond to his appeals. He would often kneel at the front of the hall or at the communion rail, having made an evangelistic appeal, and the sight of this small man kneeling in prayer, having done his bit and now waiting for the Holy Spirit to evoke a response, became familiar over the years. However many times you've done it before, there's always that agonizing wait until you become aware of first one, then another person kneeling to surrender their lives to Jesus Christ. The evangelistic service and sermon was very much a feature of the 1980s, began to lessen in the 1990s and is now much rarer. It seems that courses (*Alpha, Essence, Just Looking, Christianity Explored* etc.) have replaced the evangelistic sermon. It will be interesting to see how it gets re-invented (as it surely must!). Had Rob lived longer, he would undoubtedly have had plenty of ideas on the subject. That style of service may have become less common, but it was still so much a part of Rob's ministry that he did it whenever he was given an opportunity. He took careful heed of Paul's advice to Timothy: 'Preach the Word; be prepared in season and out of season . . .' (2 Tim. 4:2). However, Rob was much more than an evangelistic preacher.

He was a personal evangelist. Despite an enormous workload inside the church, Rob always cultivated friendships with people who weren't yet Christians and saw a good number of them become Christians. When Rob died, it was amazing the number of people who said in different ways, 'Rob was my friend.' He had a wonderful ability to come alongside people, to listen to them and befriend them. He always took people seriously where they were, and always longed for them to move on and draw closer to God.

He was a media evangelist. He loved writing columns in secular newspapers. For many years, he was the 'agony aunt' for a local free newspaper, and he linked that work into counselling which, though available to people of all faiths and none, had a distinct Christian feel to it. He also enjoyed working in both radio and television. As well as recording programmes for the Christian media, he also regularly pitched ideas to commercial television companies, always with an evangelistic edge. Of all the things he did as a preacher, a five-minute sermon on a secular television or radio programme that persuaded people to think seriously about Jesus was, in my opinion, his greatest gift. I remember the story of a man listening to Rob on the radio, pulling into a lay-by to pray a prayer asking Jesus to be his Lord and Saviour, then writing to Rob saying, 'What do I do next?'

He was a creative evangelist. From the very beginning, he realized how different people respond to different media. Evangelism that relies totally on the spoken word reaches some people but misses many others. The combination of music, drama and testimony/preaching is a much more powerful medium. Rob continually wrestled with the balance between a highly professional presentation and a sense of the anointing of the Holy Spirit. Some of the earliest presentations were strong on passion but weak on professionalism. There were a small number of events that used professional actors and musicians, but they didn't have the same sense of faith and passion as the earliest tours. Eventually Rob found a group of trusted friends and allies – including Paul Field for music and Stephen Deal for drama – who combined passion with professionalism. Rob partnered with them for many years.

Tours like the Gospel Roadshow, Daybreak, Gospel End, Visions, and Hopes and Dreams were a brilliant concept. There was a small travelling core of musicians and actors who took the leading roles and performed them to the highest standards. Each event then raised a large group of people to sing in the choir and perform fringe roles in the drama. Involving lots of local people in the cast meant that they sold tickets to family and friends, many of whom were not yet Christians. These people were not only entertained by the quality of the production, but also they heard a clear evangelistic message and were challenged to become followers of Jesus. Many local Christians were on hand to follow up those who had become Christians or who were thinking about it but not yet convinced.

The local casts could then follow on with local productions so that even more people were involved and the evangelistic impact widened. There's also something very compelling about a big event in an evangelistic context. The travelling productions mostly used large secular theatres and had audiences of several hundred people. This creates a very different dynamic to a local church event with only a small number in the audience. It makes it easier for non-Christians to come and see what the claims of Jesus are, without feeling that they're in danger of being 'put on the spot'. I have a vivid recollection of an open-air performance of 'Visions' in a park in Oldham. A noisy group of Muslim teenagers came into the park to heckle, but they were held by the music and drama and began to listen to the good news of Jesus. Only a small number of people became Christians that night, but a lot more seeds were sown – who knows what harvest they will reap?

Rob understood the spirituality of people outside church and the Christian faith. Many Christians still find it hard to believe that many people outside the church believe that they are spiritual (which is good) but churchgoers are religious (which is bad!). He was challenged and disturbed by a visit to Totnes in Devon where he found a high street full of New Age shops and a slightly dilapidated Methodist church which seemed to be totally oblivious to the outpouring of spirituality around it. After a good deal of research, he began to find ways of engaging with these new forms of spirituality. This was a difficult step for him to take because some of his traditional evangelical supporters thought he was going off the rails. The Essence course helped lots of Christians to engage with their 'spiritual' friends in a journey to find faith in Christ. It is significantly different to many of the other Christian discovery courses in that it is much more experiential, engaging all the senses – not just the ears! It also roots evangelism in the creation story rather than in a redemption story. This is not about discounting the importance of the fall and the centrality of the cross in our redemption. It's rather about starting where people are and then leading them into the Christian story.

Many of the Christian discovery courses make unhelpful assumptions about the level of Christian knowledge that people have. The relational nature of these courses to some extent counteracts the weaknesses in their content, and they have been wonderfully used by God. But Rob was keen to go further out to where people with no Christian knowledge or understanding at all would feel able to begin.

He was an apologist for Christianity and loved nothing better than wrestling with scientific and philosophical worldviews to defend and explain the Christian faith. Some people do this to win arguments – Rob did it to win converts. His natural networking skills meant that he linked up with scientists to do tours about science and faith. One of the significant advantages of this approach is that the science agenda opens far more doors in the secular world of education than religion. He was able to do tours which touched on ecology, astrophysics and other big scientific issues; there would be presentations in schools and colleges during the day, with more overtly evangelistic events in the evening.

Rob was an equipping evangelist – he didn't just do it himself, he released others into the ministry. He did this at a personal level by mentoring hundreds of (mostly young) people. On Share Jesus missions and Seed Team programmes, young people found a safe place to test out and develop their evangelistic gifts – many of them coming from churches where such gifts were not even noticed, much less encouraged. The Share Jesus mission teams in particular always had a talent-spotting role for the team leaders so that people with evangelistic gifts were nurtured and encouraged to take more prominent roles in later years. Rob was also happy to do this in a systemic way. The travelling productions were always designed so that local churches could take what they had seen done in a professional way and adapt it for a local production. Share Jesus missions were regularly visited by Christian leaders from other countries who were interested in learning how the concept worked. The biggest 'export market' for Share Jesus was the USA, where a small number of us travelled to both California and Florida to help local Christians launch similar programmes.

How do you define an evangelist? The bottom line is simple – an evangelist is someone around whom people become Christians. By this definition Rob was a brilliant evangelist. Evangelism was his defining passion – he went about it in lots of different ways. Paul was speaking of himself, but he could just as easily have been speaking of Rob when he said:

> Though I am free and belong to no man, I make myself a slave to everyone, to win as many as possible. To the Jews I became like a Jew, to win the Jews. To those under the law I became like one under the law (though I myself am not under the law), so as to win those under the law. To those not having the law I became like one not having the law (though I am not free from God's law but am under Christ's law), so as to win those not having the law. To the weak I became weak, to win the weak. I have become all things to all men so that by all possible means I might save some.
>
> (1 Cor. 9:19–22)

Rob as a Radio DJ

Tony Miles,
Presenter on Premier Radio's 'Big Breakfast'

Picture a scene in the days before television. A tiny baby Robert bouncing on his mother's knee in Sowerby Bridge, Halifax, intrigued and delighted by the sounds coming out of a little box. This must have been the beginning of Rob's fascination with radio.

Later, in the early 1960s, when his dad, Ron, was serving as a minister in Plymouth, young Rob would occasionally get permission to stay up late. This was to enable him to accompany his dad as he gave the epilogue for Westward TV. This was in the very early days of television, when Westward was the first ITV franchise holder for the South-West of England. 'The Unsleeping Sword' was in the schedule as a devotional conclusion after the last nightly news bulletin and before closedown. Rob's mother affectionately called it the 'Dozy Dagger'! It all took place in a little room, with Ron sitting on one side of a desk and the newsreader opposite him, in view of the camera. To give the impression of being in a bigger studio, however, the newsreader and the minister would exchange places whilst the camera was momentarily focused on the weather map. They would crawl under the table whilst pulling a curtain across to make it look as though Ron was elsewhere. Rob thought this was a hoot and found the bizarre ritual captivating. No wonder broadcasting became an early preoccupation. This was one of his first lessons in 'shoestring broadcasting'. He always wanted to get the most out of the money spent, the equipment available and the time to be filled!

After doing well at Bournville College of Further Education in Birmingham, Rob wanted to go into the broadcasting industry. He saved up his money to buy his first camera – which he later sold in order to respond to a call to become a preacher and go to Cliff College. This could have been the end of Rob's involvement in broadcasting, but his love for the medium and his interest in its potential led him to use it as a tool and a hobby, later in his ministry.

In this respect, Rob and I had similar journeys of faith. In fact, he counselled me when I first considered giving up running a mobile discotheque and abandoning hospital radio, in order to respond to my call to the Methodist ministry. Rob was such a good friend; he had time for people and was genuinely interested in their spiritual journeys. He encouraged me to be very sure about my call before I made my decision, just in case God wanted to use me in the media, rather than the ministry. Nevertheless, it became very clear to me that I was called towards ordination, so he urged me not to forget the natural gifts God had given me concerning communication, entertainment and popular music. With Rob, encouraging others wasn't just a matter of words; he frequently backed up his belief and confidence in me, and others, with action. He created opportunities for me to become more involved in broadcasting, roping me into his various projects to nurture my potential whilst helping him out. It was fun!

Radio was a passion we shared – it gave us both a tremendous buzz. It was mostly lost on our wives, but Rob and I had a mutual understanding concerning the opportunities and possibilities of radio. He loved sharing stories, with belly laughs, over a coffee or breakfast, about the times when things went pear-shaped (which they did frequently), or the times when they went surprisingly well (thank the Lord!). We also enjoyed simply letting off steam after broadcasts, reliving this show or that interview. I think Rob would admit that he was a true 'radio anorak'!

The word 'broadcast' is full of biblical imagery from the Parable of the Sower (Matt. 13:1–23). It literally means 'to cast broadly'. In many respects, this sums up the whole of Rob's ministry. He took every opportunity, in obedience to the Holy

Spirit, to sow the seed of God's word broadly. Rob loved Jesus with all of his heart and simply gave himself to enabling others to love him too, and to know the power of his saving grace in their lives. His use of radio and television was an effective means to this end. Just as John Wesley went outside the churches to where people worked and to the market-places, so Rob went to where they were using broadcast technology. This is something I'm sure John Wesley would have done, if presented with the same opportunities – much to the relief of his horse!

One example of Rob seeing the potential of radio was when he challenged Simon Parnall to set up a special radio service for the yearly Christian conference, Easter People. Previously, EP had been held at a holiday camp in Camber Sands and he'd used closed-circuit television to transmit information and celebrations to people in their chalets. However, once EP moved out from the closed confines of a holiday camp to become an event and mission in a town, Rob wanted to unite those attending. People were staying in hotels, B&Bs, self-catering apartments, caravans and kibbutzes, and Rob wanted everyone to know what was going on, and he hoped that the locals might tune in too! Whilst he would speak on the radio, be interviewed, and give his thoughts, he didn't want to be a programme-maker himself. EP Radio was part of something bigger and he delegated the job of programming and running the outfit to others. This was another of Rob's great gifts and it also demonstrated his trust. He was an enabler who placed a frightening amount of confidence in his friends – especially young leaders. Countless people have found their way into full-time Christian ministry, or into some kind of Christian service or mission, through Rob. He recognized people's gifts, but he also entrusted them with huge amounts of responsibility. He was committed to people sharing in his vision, in order for it to become a reality.

EP Radio developed over many years, expanding to more than one site, with links that allowed Rob to speak to everyone simultaneously – even enabling both congregations to jointly participate in a morning service on Radio Four. Simon Parnall writes:

One of my particular highlights was the year when we transmitted speech and music from the band on the bus, using a radio link back to the station, and then on to the mass crowds walking the streets, with radio receivers from our hilltop transmitter. A total of three links, all working together to make this a March for Jesus where everyone was singing together. It's been done since, but I am pretty convinced that we were the first to try this. Made possible because Rob was prepared to back our ideas with his (sometimes) childlike enthusiasm.

I'm sure this was partly because he just loved the whole idea of using radio. It was a great privilege to be involved with EP Radio. It was hugely demanding on the radio team, but it gave us an opportunity to develop our presenting skills and make mistakes in a safe environment and forgiving fellowship.

Simon Parnall gives a further illustration of how Rob was an enabler:

> For me, EP Radio was the precursor to Radio Cracker in Wimbledon, a project that I led for two years; and which was, incidentally, for both years the station that generated the most income. I was the station manager, Clive Jones the chairman of our project and Rob, living locally, was very much involved in the project too – conducting interviews, on-air services each week, and on-air thoughts throughout each month-long operation. He helped to sustain us spiritually, as an encourager and as someone who took what we were doing very seriously indeed. That was a tremendous blessing to us all.

After EP Radio and Radio Cracker came Peter Meadow's vision of London Christian Radio. Rob was involved from the outset through to the launch of Premier. Why? Rob said simply, 'I want to bless London.' Naturally, he was given a programme, initially on a Sunday evening at the first home for the Premier studios. This was a challenge! Rob may have done some radio before, but he needed a strong team to get him through and to create a show and playlist around his constant supply of guests. Rob may have been a good presenter, but he would freely admit that the equipment and technical side of things was not his forte. He would be completely stumped if he had to 'put the bonnet up'! His team was a great support to Rob for his first two years at Premier. Despite their frustrations with him at times and their arrivals home at two or three o'clock on Monday mornings, they had fun and they enabled Rob to hone his skills and get the best out of his guests.

In Premier's early days, Rob was also more than a presenter. He became the station's unofficial chaplain. During a turbulent time for Premier Radio, Rob was there for many who were either made redundant or who found their roles changing. He always had the heart of a pastor and loved people. He'd listen, encourage and pray with people, as required. This was all on top of his demanding schedule and without complaint.

When Peter Kerridge became Premier's station manager, he wanted Rob to be able to drive the Premier Desk himself and not rely on his team so heavily. This wasn't what Rob wanted. He wanted to concentrate on interviewing his guests and talking to the audience. Nevertheless, he undertook the necessary training. Gary Birch had the daunting task of teaching Rob how to 'fly solo'. The ever-patient Gary comments with generous affection:

Rob wasn't the most technically co-ordinated person and would always leave his microphone up when going into a track or the adverts, and so you would hear him talk to, or worse still, talk about his guests to those in the studio! He also liked to 'crash' the news, either entering in too early or late! What I loved about Rob, though, was that he rarely let any of these technical issues worry him! He'd just carry on, ever the professional, while us 'techies' would try to keep everything working! I loved working with Rob – a complete nightmare but much fun.

Rob's programme was then moved to Sunday morning and became Premier's flagship show, *Frost on Sunday*.

Some years previously, Revd Dr Peter Graves had been the minister of Epsom Methodist Church, Rob had been an associate minister at the same church, and I had been their Lay Pastoral Assistant (whilst candidating for the Methodist ministry). How strange that a few years into Premier's life, the three of us became part of the station's programming, having all been approached separately! Rob was delighted to hear the news that I was to co-present on Saturday mornings from October 1997. Throughout my time at Premier he kept in touch and shared ideas, concerns, opportunities and potential guests. He'd often ring me on a Saturday morning to say that he was listening and I was doing a good job, and 'One more thing, mate, whilst I'm on the line. Could I just do a live plug for . . .?' How could I resist? There was also a surprise one Christmas morning, when I was presenting *The Big Breakfast* with the assistance of my family. We had risen at 5.30 a.m., driven to London and set up the show, and all whilst I was suffering from a sudden bout of flu. I was heavily relying on my family and soldiering on, when suddenly a cheery Rob arrived in the studio to encourage us. He gave us all a hug, wished us a happy Christmas, thanked us for all we were doing and said a prayer. It was so uplifting and we'll never forget it. 'Oh, and one more thing, mate, whilst I'm here. Could I just do a live plug for . . . ?' And I let him!

Rob's interviewing and technical skills developed and *Frost on Sunday* drew a vast listenership. I'm sure he held the record for the largest number of guests a single presenter has ever had on one show! Each week, with the help of his producers, he would trawl through his contacts and databases and find friends to come and talk about this or that issue. He would always put his guests at ease – despite being under pressure himself. One disconcerting habit he adopted was shutting his eyes when he asked you a question. This was his way of concentrating, but you were never sure if he was listening or catching up with some sleep! Toby Scott, co-head of communication for the Methodist Church of Great Britain, writes:

> Rob managed to keep a two-hour show flowing with guests, regulars and sometimes their children moving in and out without it ever once collapsing in chaos. Live radio always terrifies me, but he was at home with it and knew, from years of experience and hard work, how to make it work both as radio and as Christian broadcasting.

Jonathan Green, a pastor working with young adults, comments:

Rob would always brief us in the studio about where he was going in the next section, and then two minutes later he would go in a completely different and sometimes 'random' direction. I loved his style and his questions – they were so insightful and often very funny. I was on his Sunday show two weeks before his death. He didn't once mention his health but asked after me and my family.

Rob always seemed to be available to broadcast at times of tragedy. This happened on numerous occasions at Premier. Richard Smith tells of what happened on the morning of Sunday, 31 August 1997. Having woken up, he put the radio on:

I couldn't make out why there was so much sombre music until there was a news flash about the death of Diana, Princess of Wales. I was on a Share Jesus mission and sleeping in Pontypridd in the team house. I found some of the team around the television. 'Where's Rob?' I asked. 'Oh, he's rushed off to London for Premier.' We couldn't listen to him in South Wales, but we did get a garbled message from him later that he would be on the air all morning and hopefully back on mission around 2 p.m., having caught a late morning train from Paddington. I went down to Cardiff Central station at 2.15 p.m. when the train was due. Rob was not on that train, but we discovered that he would be back around 4 p.m. Rob eventually arrived and was absolutely exhausted. He had been broadcasting all morning, ringing up all the major church and government leaders to get comments. As usual, he maintained his high standard of presentation.

This was typically Rob, who did it to serve Premier, the listeners, and his Lord – never for his own glory!

Rob also loved what we call OBs (Outside Broadcasts). Sometimes these were literally outside in the open air, but on other occasions Rob used his connections to present *Frost on Sunday* from wherever he happened to be in the world. These occasions were highly stressful for his technicians, but somehow (God was obviously on his side!) Rob always managed to pull things off – albeit at the very last minute.

I should add that Rob didn't just broadcast for Premier; he worked with other Christian broadcasters, such as UCB, and had been a well-respected contributor to many secular radio stations at home and overseas. I believe he even put a programme proposal to Kelvin Mackenzie when he created a consortium to take over Talk Radio (Kelvin, that is, not Rob!). Olave Snelling, a former Premier presenter, says:

> Rob was super-intelligent and had such a quick brain to take in and analyse the substance of the most contentious of issues and the ability to go to the nub of the matter in the most complex political, spiritual or sociological conundrums. He could mix with the 'great and the good' on their intellectual level because he was up there on a par with them. He had a passionate nature but a very controlled expression of it so that what he said always had the feel of being tempered by the filter of the Holy Spirit. His arguments were always very well reasoned but he was never afraid to challenge error vigorously and with passion.

I must end by expressing my love to Rob's family – especially Jacqui, Andy, Chris, and Rob's father, Ron. They were all a great strength and inspiration to him – especially Jacqui!

I also thank God that Rob leaves a legacy of changed lives, challenged churches and renewed Christian institutions. I thank God for his passion for evangelism and communicating the Christian faith, flowing from his deep love for the Lord. I thank God that he was a man of prayer and conviction, who courageously pursued what God was saying to him, despite his relentless itinerary and personal exhaustion at times. Thousands, possibly millions, of people have been influenced spiritually by this faithful Methodist, whose ministry went far beyond his denomination. He stood up for what he believed to be true, constantly challenging comfortable Christianity.

Yet, despite his fame, Rob was a humble man and a good friend to many. He will be greatly missed, but we know he's now enjoying all that his Father (the great Producer), Jesus (the Word) and the Holy Spirit (of Creativity) have in store for him.

The challenge: Rob would want you, and I, to take up the baton and continue the task of broadcasting the gospel in imaginative and proactive ways – wherever we find ourselves and wherever people can be found. I believe this is the living tribute Rob would want from us!

A prayer

O loving God,
you call us to follow Jesus and to serve you in the world;
you inspire and sustain us, whilst equipping us for service.
Yet, you never promised that our lives would be easy!
Your promise was to be with us as we walk our sometimes
    difficult journey of faith.
We give you thanks for the dedicated life of Rob Frost,
for his total Christian commitment and love of you;
for his humility and courage;
for his obedience and passion in communicating the saving power
    of Jesus;
for the way he helped others into a relationship with you through
    our Lord;
for his ability to release people's gifts and share the vision you
    gave to him.
We continue to pray for his family and close friends –
especially his wife, Jacqui,
his children, Andy and Chris,
and his father, Ron.
Bless, keep and comfort them,
and enfold them in your everlasting arms of love.
May they hold onto all the wonderful promises that Rob believed
    with all his heart,
and through their tears, may they be assured of the joy of eternal
    life,
through Jesus Christ, our only Saviour and Lord. Amen.

Rob as a TV Broadcaster

Howard Ross,
TV producer

My friendship with Rob started innocently enough many years ago. At the time I was a television producer working on an idiosyncratic mix of situation comedies, recorded – as if live – in front of a large studio audience, and current affairs programmes transmitted live each week. So it didn't seem odd to be asked to add to this gallimaufry the broadcasts of the Sunday morning Acts of Worship which were a staple of religious output at the time by both the BBC and ITV.

The time-honoured format I inherited for these weekly live outside broadcasts was a decorous mix of traditional canonical liturgy illustrated by shots of the spruced-up congregation, a luminescent choir, soft-focus images of stained-glass windows and guttering candles, all periodically dissolving into committee-designed flower arrangements and spring-cleaned fluted Corinthian columns. It was all very pretty and very cosy but unchallenging, most certainly not controversial, and adding very little to the act of worship itself. Even though these programmes undoubtedly had a devoted following, it seemed to me that they represented only one aspect of a new, exciting and developing gamut of worship which I knew was taking place across the nation.

For some months I carried on the traditional output, all the while seeking out and compiling a list of interesting people and visiting all sorts of venues to observe faith in action, not stagnating behind studded oak doors and Gothic walls.

My research very soon pointed me towards an energetic, enthusiastic, exciting man called Rob Frost. Coincidentally, at roughly the same time it seems he was pointed towards me. We met – for lunch, I think – in Waterloo. I immediately warmed to him. He was bursting with ideas. He presented me with a flood of suggestions which would have sunk even Noah. Eventually we decided that a proposal for an open-air service – comparatively rare in those days – particularly appealed to both of us. I shouldn't really call it a 'service' – it was more of an event. I very soon discovered that everything Rob did was an event or, perhaps more accurately termed, a 'happening'!

For the broadcast Rob chose a grassy knoll which overlooked a natural amphitheatre in a remote park in south London. I approached my religious advisers at the time – each of them appointed by the major Christian denominations.

'It sounds too unstructured. What's he going to do?' they asked.

'I'm not sure,' I replied, 'but it sounds exciting to me and I trust him to deliver.'

I approached my technical advisers. 'You won't need lights so it'll be cheaper than usual. Good! But what's your wet weather cover?' they enquired.

'God and Rob!' I replied.

Television technology wasn't as sophisticated then as it is today. The outside broadcast cameras were heavy, not easily manoeuvrable and attached to a central control vehicle by metres of umbilical cables which took a squad of strong men many hours to lay out. Not such a problem in a church – but up and down grassy banks in the middle of a park . . . ! Generally my crew thought I was mad. The cameramen weren't quite so worried – after all, they'd be coming straight on from covering a live football match the Saturday afternoon before. They reckoned that if they could spot the ball through pouring rain, they could certainly capture a vicar in a dog-collar. The sound engineers, I seem to remember, said it was a recipe for disaster and it definitely wouldn't work.

On the day the congregation – all bussed in – sat on the very damp grass. The almost predictable rain which fell the night before had, eventually, stopped!

With no time for rehearsal, the transmission began. By a lake below the knoll a band played and sang, readers popped up from seemingly anywhere and people gave their testimony from everywhere. Amongst it all Rob wandered around willy-nilly and largely unscripted. Needless to say, even though there was no dog-collar in sight, neither cameras nor sound missed a single moment of a very original broadcast held together by Rob, who drove the show seamlessly from beginning to end. And judging by the abundance of letters we received afterwards, it was a resounding success too with the majority of the audience viewing at home.

So began my long working partnership with Rob and, more importantly, our strong and lasting friendship.

On another occasion in our working relationship, Rob and I decided we'd like to do the Remembrance Sunday broadcast. We couldn't go to the Cenotaph, as the BBC had the monopoly there – and anyway, would the Queen be willing to adapt to Rob's vision for the day? So, after much discussion, we decided we'd go to Enniskillen in Northern Ireland in remembrance of the bomb that had been detonated at the War Memorial there. We visited the town in the planning process and talked to everyone, seeking and getting cooperation from all the contentious factions. Proud though Rob was at achieving this rapprochement, there was still something missing: 'Everyone's going to be tuned in to the Cenotaph,' he said to me. What could we do to match the Queen in Whitehall?

I can't remember who came up with the idea of Princess Diana, but as soon as it was suggested, Rob was on the phone and ere long she was 'booked'. Rob had a way with him which meant that NO ONE could say no to him once he set his mind to something.

The Princess of Wales duly turned up in Enniskillen and it was planned that she would read from the Beatitudes. The only problem was that at the very last minute she had to answer a call of nature and, in a very tightly scheduled programme – we had to hit eleven o'clock on the dot for the two minutes' silence – there suddenly wasn't time to put a radio microphone on her. A microphone on a stand was hurriedly placed in the relevant position, but unfortunately the cable was accidentally disconnected just as she started to speak. My only source of sound was from Rob's lapel microphone. I recall screaming into his earpiece: 'Get closer to her, Rob! Closer still! Even closer!' I have this abiding image of Rob – not the tallest of men – tucking himself under the bosom of the Princess as he attempted to pick up her voice for me on his microphone.

Yes, I doubt if the Queen would have been amused if that had happened at the Cenotaph. But then she probably wasn't amused the following day either when she opened the morning newspapers to discover that the Princess of Wales in Enniskillen had stolen the headlines. Rob was, needless to say, delighted.

But Rob was always delighted with anything to do with television. In his youth he had been fascinated by the medium and for a few adolescent years he had fully intended to enter the broadcasting industry, before he heard the call to serve God as a Methodist minister. I have no doubt that if he'd continued with his boyhood dreams he would have achieved great things and, by now, television would be quite different and very much better.

Over the years Rob rang me often, excited by the latest long list of ideas he had for television and radio programmes – and I did the same to him. Together we pitched ideas to heads of religious departments and commissioning editors.

Rob was never happier than when he was combining his two great loves – broadcasting and his faith – and he was always determinedly striving to get the message of God across to a wider constituency. He recognized that his ministry demanded much more from him than preaching to the already converted – he wanted ever greater numbers of people to understand and live by the word of God. The way of reaching those people, we both firmly believed, was to bravely release religious programming from the protective ghetto of mid-morning and early-evening Sundays – slots which we believed were likely to disappear before long anyway – and onto mainstream television at peak times. However, to achieve this transition, the presentation of the programmes needed to be appealing, interesting, exciting, entertaining and relevant, and compete fairly and squarely for the attention of a broad audience. Without this approach the programmes wouldn't deserve to get into the schedules. This all required vision from religious leaders and increased budgets from broadcasting managements. Neither was forthcoming and religious broadcasting has, as we predicted, largely disappeared from the terrestrial channels.

Eventually I did less and less television and returned to my first love – the theatre. Rob and I talked often of getting together on a theatre project, but sadly, that was never to be.

Meanwhile Rob found a niche making programmes for the God Channel. He made a number of series, all of which were highly successful. I didn't participate in those programmes with him but he would invariably call me and tell me of his latest project, and we continued to meet often and throw around crazy ideas.

The next time we really worked together on a project was on Premier Christian Radio. Rob was involved with Premier from the very beginning, and he rang me to say that he had a late-night weekend slot on the station, and would I like to come along and observe? I should have known that he didn't mean 'observe' in the dictionary sense – it was his way of saying, 'Come along and be part of it!'

Thus began our regular weekly late-night gigs at Premier Radio's first studio in Victoria. That original studio was quite compact – a polite way of saying small – and microphone outputs were in short supply. This, of course, meant that we had to limit the number of guests we could have in the studio at any one time. But we didn't! Each week the studio would be full to capacity and beyond, with microphones being constantly swung from one person to another . . . to another . . . and to yet another. When the studio was full of standing guests – there was no room for non-speaking chairs! – a roving microphone on a long length of cable would be run to an adjoining room or a corridor or an office. You'd think we were attempting to gain entry into *The Guinness Book of Records* for the number of bodies you can get into a radio studio at any one time – and we'd have got the entry too!

The broadcast would start with a pre-planned structure, but that would quickly disappear. I'd try to keep a hold on

the programme by either talking directly into Rob's head-
phones with suggestions as to where the discussion might go
next, or typing questions up onto a screen in front of him or,
as a last resort, somehow squeezing through the studio
guests and passing on a hand-scribbled note to him. It was
both exciting and exhausting and, needless to say, Rob was in
his element.

When the Premier programme was moved to a Sunday
morning, Rob asked me, along with others, to review the
morning newspapers. The first time I did it, I went out late on
the Saturday night for the early editions and devoured them in
great detail, working out exactly what I was going to talk
about. I arrived in the studio fully prepared. Rob greeted me
and said, 'Talk about what's in the papers . . . but can you also
bring in such-and-such a subject, as I've got a guest in the studio and he's a specialist in . . . whatever-it-happened-to-be.' I
knew there was nothing in any of the Sunday papers about
that subject and I only had a very brief memory of having read
something about it during the week. I sent off the librarian in
my head to dredge up from the lower reaches of my mind my
recollection of the story, and then I sat in front of the microphone and quoted from memory what the papers had said earlier in the week, for Rob to then take it further with the expert
guest. I'm sure others who have reviewed the papers have
been faced with the same last-minute appeal from Rob – and
how could any of us turn him down?

'Thanks, mate,' he always said afterwards.

'That's all right, Rob – no problem,' I always replied.

I've had so many radio adventures with Rob that it's hard
to know which to tell. For instance, there was the Sunday
when, between my leaving home and arriving at the studio,
there had been a military coup somewhere or other. I walked
into the studio and Rob told me he had just set up a telephone interview with someone in the middle of the embat-
tled country – but he didn't know anything about the area, so
could I, with my knowledge of current affairs, take the lead
in the interview? Well, I hadn't yet read the newsflash and I
wasn't even sure where this place was anyway, as my current
affairs background didn't include anything about that part of

the globe. But you couldn't say no to Rob, so, somehow, you did it.

'Thanks, mate!' he once again said afterwards.

'That's all right, Rob – no problem.'

I recall that on another occasion, because of transport problems I arrived a few minutes before we went on air. There were no other guests in the studio when I walked in at the beginning of the broadcast. I wasn't worried by this, as Rob was expecting to do a telephone interview immediately after I'd done my introductory scan through the newspaper headlines. I guessed that by then the other contributors would have arrived, and they would come into the studio while I went out and swotted up on a more detailed analysis of the papers for later in the programme. We went on air. Rob announced what was coming up and introduced me for what I expected to be about a two-minute contribution. As I read out the headline stories Rob disappeared under the studio desk, popped back up again, and then rose from his chair and walked out of the studio. One eye watched him leave as my other eye continued to read the headline stories.

I finished the headlines. He didn't return. I kept talking . . . and talking . . . and talking . . . desperately scanning page after page for the very first time.

After what seemed an eternity, Rob eventually came back into the studio, sat down and indicated that he was ready to take over. I'd done a ten-minute monologue.

'Thanks, mate,' he said. 'Technical glitch with the phone interview, and I went to see what had happened to the other guests.'

'That's all right, Rob – no problem!'

When Rob died we were working together again on a series of broadcasts for Premier Radio entitled 'Burning Questions'. By this time Rob wasn't very well at all and he brought me in to prepare a list of questions and briefing notes on the major topics in the news for discussion with the distinguished guests he'd invited to be on the panels each week. In the programme Rob would ask them to explain how their faith influenced their judgement on the most diverse of topics. It was both revealing and rewarding for all concerned. At the end of each programme he said to each one of them: 'Thanks.' I'm sure they all replied: 'That's all right, Rob – no problem.'

I have many happy and often amusing memories of the years when Rob and I knew each other and worked together. I want to emphasize just how much I learnt to love and to trust him. He never let me down. He trusted each and every one of us too. He surrounded us all with his love and his friendship and, most important of all, with his faith. His faith in us made our faith in ourselves stronger each time we were in Rob's company.

Rob, what a joy you were to work with. What fun we had. Ever since that first meeting in Waterloo, we became not just colleagues but firm friends. We shared many exciting times together both in front of the camera and, more recently, behind the microphone at Premier Radio. We shared even happier times together as devoted friends. We saw a lot of each other in your last months on earth, and I was humbled to share with your family your very last hour in this world.

A great visionary, you weren't happy unless you were pushing boundaries.

You were a true friend who was always there for me when things were tough. I tried to be there when things were at their toughest for you.

Rob, I'm sure you are now in heaven happily running the BBC – the Blessed Broadcasting Corporation – asking the impossible of some poor producer. I miss you every single day, Rob. Life is not the same without you, my dear, dear friend. *Au revoir.*

And, thanks mate.

Rob as a Methodist

Martyn Turner,
Superintendent of Westminster Central Hall

Rob Frost was born into a Methodist family, cradled in Methodism, converted in Methodism, trained and ordained in Methodism, and served as a Methodist minister until his untimely death.

Those were Rob's roots, but it is also true to say that Rob struggled with Methodism as his ministry blossomed. As Paul Smith (now following in Rob's father Ron's footsteps as the Superintendent Minister of Plymouth Methodist Central Hall) has said, it was a 'love-hate relationship', and Methodism itself also often found it hard to cope with Rob.

Rob was blessed with godly parents. Even when he was just a few months old his mother would take him with her on her preaching appointments, whilst his father was the minister at some of the largest and liveliest Central Missions in Methodism. Prayer was a part of life, and the fine example of his parents made a great and lasting mark upon him. As a small boy Rob was part of the Sunday School at Plymouth, where a teacher remembers him as being quite serious and reserved.

Growing up in a Christian home does not guarantee faith, however, and for Rob the key place on his spiritual journey was the Alvechurch youth camp, organized by the Birmingham Central Hall, of which Ron Frost was by then the minister. Camp one year started Rob thinking, and then after a slow spiritual journey of a further year, his faith became real as, on Easter Sunday, he heard an elderly Methodist deaconess preach, and everything slipped into place. After lunch he went into the woods to be alone, and there he prayed and committed his life to Christ. Methodism had played the key role of midwife in Rob's spiritual birth!

Rob had then expected to pursue studies and a career within the media, but increasingly wondered if this was right, and a meeting with some Cliff College (the Methodist Lay Evangelism Training Centre) students set him thinking. He applied there and was accepted for the year 1969–70. As Rob himself wrote, 'The year at Cliff College was inspiring. It was definitely a watershed in my life.' Rob met his close friend Bob Kitching there, and Bob also speaks of Cliff being a formative experience for Rob. Both Bob and another Cliff friend, Barrie Morris, remember the Principal, Howard Belben, saying to them that Rob was the student with the most visionary potential of any he had taught – how right he was! Rob was one of the youngest students at Cliff, but when the ten 'Trek' teams were formed to set off for their four-week missions up and down the country, Rob was chosen as a leader. He was one of the youngest Trek leaders ever chosen – this shows the great faith that Howard Belben had in Rob. On another occasion Belben said, 'This young man has great qualities of leadership. One day he will make an impact on the church.' A further thing Rob did whilst at Cliff was to recruit students to help with his father's summer camps at Alvechurch, and for six years Rob and others from Cliff worked at the camps, serving deprived children from the Birmingham slums.

An interesting story told by his friend Robin Searles shows Rob's loyalty to Methodism. Robin was balancing the Elim Bible College against Methodist training, and the former looked very attractive to him. Rob knew of his thinking, and a note came under Robin's door quoting St Paul: 'If we all leave the ship it will sink.'

By now Rob himself had a strong call to the Methodist ministry. As was the custom in those days, he went to spend a year working in a church whilst candidating. He went to Deptford Mission, then under the dynamic leadership of Roy Dew – a man to whom Rob always felt a great debt of gratitude. Robin Searles, who was working just across the Thames, tells of the time when Rob wanted to excite and challenge the children in his youth club, and decided they should put on a special Palm Saturday event. One of the Deptford lads had long hair, so Rob made him Jesus! This young man was persuaded to ride a donkey down Deptford High Street, followed by children waving palm branches and shouting 'Follow, follow, I will follow Jesus!' There was also the promise that the local newspaper would be there to take their picture.

On the day, the lad who was to play Jesus was so thrilled about being in the local paper that he had his hair cut; the donkey was unavailable, so the local rag and bone man came and 'Jesus' sat up alongside him as the horse and cart led the procession; and the photographer waited on the wrong street, so there was no picture – a story with a certain familiarity to those of us who worked with Rob over the years!

Rob had met his theology tutor Dick Jones prior to arriving at Hartley Victoria College. Rob had been leading a mission at Newquay with some friends, and on the final Sunday morning he told the story of Jonah with such over-the-top theatrical gusto that even his team were embarrassed! One of the holidaymakers introduced himself and his family – it was Dick Jones. Rob mentioned that he would soon be going to Hartley Victoria College, to which Dick replied, 'That's very interesting. I will be teaching you some theology!'

Rob made lifelong friends at Hartley. One of them, Bob Kitching, writes: 'To some extent Rob was a maverick at college, revelling in college life but also being no mean student intellectually.' It was at Hartley that I met Rob for the first time. I told him I was hoping to candidate (that is, to apply to train as a Methodist minister), and he left me in no doubt at all about what a hard time I would have as an evangelical, both in candidating and at college – perhaps that reflected his own experience! It was whilst on mission from Hartley that Rob met Jacqui, his future wife, a creative person whose gifts and vision were equal to and helpfully complemented Rob's.

After College came stationing, first to South Emsall in the Pontefract Circuit (1975–8). There he did great work, especially with the young people, and whilst he was there he was ordained at the 1977 Hull Conference. Then he moved to

Mitcham in South London, where his successor John Haley spoke of taking over a church which 'had been transformed from a dying suburban congregation into a lively and expectant evangelical community'.

It was whilst he was at Mitcham, however, that he became restive. His then Chair of District, Colin Rowe, writes:

> I sensed that although he was a diligent, faithful minister who served his people effectively and looked out for evangelical opportunities of outreach, nevertheless it was not a sphere in which he was really happy. He wanted to be out and about with the gospel. He very clearly felt the call to be an evangelist and to use his skills on a larger plain. He was convinced that was where God wanted him to be.

Rob was indeed fortunate to have such a flexible and forward-thinking Chairman as Colin Rowe. The two of them went to see the General Secretary of the Home Mission Division, Donald English. Donald lived locally, so they went round one evening to discuss matters, finishing with a time of prayer and the agreement that Donald and Colin would go to the Stationing Committee and seek permission for Rob to be freed to be a connexional evangelist. Colin writes: 'We did not have an easy time but Donald was at his best and finally permission was given.' It is fair to say that from then on, Donald English played a very significant role in enabling, supporting and affirming Rob in all that he did, whilst Colin Rowe chaired Rob's first Steering Group. Rob was blessed to have the support of two such fine senior ministers. For Rob, Jacqui and the family, the new role meant a move to a fairly small house in Cheam, whilst Rob had a small but key team of administrators and actors working with him as various projects developed.

The breadth of Rob's spirituality and thinking is shown in the themes of these projects. 'Breaking Bread', with its emphasis on the liturgy of Holy Communion, put Rob firmly in the tradition of the Wesley brothers. 'Pilgrims' was essentially a prayer walk, allowing people to experience a new form of spirituality linked to the Celtic tradition. Some events were more like a theatre visit, while others were more like a traditional evangelical evening rally. However, in all of them the common theme was Rob's concern for the empowerment of ordinary Methodists. His touring Roadshows nearly always needed a local team of singers and actors, and the capacity to adapt and use his ideas locally showed how ready Rob was to give away his creative work for the good of the Kingdom.

Sometimes Rob's enthusiasm and vision meant that he unwittingly got across the local Methodist establishment figures. Rob would organize events without any reference to local Circuit or District officers; in particular, his relationships with the Youth Department became strained. However, the success of the events and Rob's fulsome and gracious apologies always won the day, and in time Rob's work was valued more and more.

Most significant of all for Methodism, however, was the creation of Easter People in 1987. Rob was concerned that there was little for the more evangelical Methodists to attend other than events such as Spring Harvest, where a Methodist presence on the speaking teams was almost totally lacking. He faced a considerable battle getting Connexional Methodism to support his venture, and tells of the concept being turned down by no fewer than five national committees and boards! Rob was, however, convinced that this was a vision from God, so he battled on and went back to each of the national bodies, and eventually each of them changed their mind and offered support. He therefore called together a leadership group, largely Methodists, and the event was launched at a holiday camp at Camber Sands, with Donald English coming as the main attraction, as he led magnificent Bible studies. All this happened with the blessing and encouragement of Spring Harvest. Although Easter People was always avowedly ecumenical, the vast majority there in these early years were rooted in Methodism, and most of those taking responsibility and doing the work were also Methodists. Rob saw Easter People as an opportunity to launch gifted Methodist speakers on to a larger canvas. This gave many the opportunity to use their gifts for the first time, and it also gave many ministers an outlet from the constraints of a traditional Methodist church. As his friend Robin Searles writes: 'I will always remember Rob for the opportunities he gave to "ordinary" circuit

Methodist ministers to take the "big stage" when at the same time Spring Harvest were using the "big names"!' I think many regretted that, as Easter People grew, the celebrity speaker culture crept in a little, with big names coming in from other denominations whilst the Methodists kept the whole thing afloat by their hard work!

The impact of Easter People on Methodism can hardly be measured. It held huge numbers in the denomination at a time when those at the more conservative end of the spectrum were thinking of leaving for pastures new. I would guess that hundreds of Methodist ministers received their call to service at Easter People. Local churches found renewal through members attending, and in time Connexional Methodism gave a firm blessing as Rob invited the President and Vice President to attend each year. After twenty years it had run its course, but I firmly believe that the impact of Easter People is one of the most significant parts of Methodist history in the late twentieth century.

In 1989 Rob and Jacqui moved into a Connexionally owned manse in Raynes Park – a far more suitably-sized house as a base for his family and work. There again, his commitment to ordinary Methodism was made plain as the family got involved with the local church, and shared in launching alternative-style café worship. Nearly twenty years later, this church was also the venue for Rob's funeral service.

National restructuring within Methodism meant that Rob was working in the 'Church and Society' team, and I think it is fair to say that he was less comfortable in that team than he had been in Home Mission. A more formal management structure was also set up at this time. Again, Rob did not always sit comfortably with it. The Chair, Revd Martyn Broadbent, found that 'managing' Rob was an impossible task. He said on one occasion: 'Rob has three good ideas before breakfast most days, and a brilliant one almost every month!'

In 2001 Share Jesus International was formed, and Rob now had an ecumenical rather than a Methodist base – although Methodism continued to provide the Raynes Park Manse. As Brian Hoare, for some years Rob's line manager at Home Missions, writes: 'At the end of the day he was too big for any denominational strait-jacket, and was always happier when he was able to work both within and beyond the Methodist Church with those who shared his passion for evangelism.' At a Connexional level Rob sat on many boards and committees and was a faithful servant of his church. As one of the most influential leaders within Methodism for a quarter of a century, it was both sad and surprising that Methodism never honoured him by calling him to be President. Some just did not like Rob – his theology and his style. Others loved him dearly but felt he would be constrained by the formality and role of President. Many of those outside the somewhat rarefied air of Conference just could not understand why the one minister they knew at a national level never made it to the office where he could have made such an immense contribution. Rob himself was keen to become President – not out of pride but because of the platform that would give for evangelism. He attended Conference fairly regularly but never really came to understand it, often sitting looking glum and making somewhat over-strong or badly timed contributions. How sad, however, that Methodism could not have had more grace and recognized and honoured one of her most loyal and effective ministers.

So if we try to sum up Rob Frost the Methodist, we see a man who was indeed Methodist to the core, but the Methodism which Rob loved and was loyal to was the Methodism of the Wesleys and the Methodism of the evangelical mission hall. He had little time for what he regarded as the theologically liberal, weak and anaemic establishment of the church he served in. He was a keen supporter of the Methodist Revival Fellowship and Conservative Evangelicals in Methodism, continuing his support with considerable enthusiasm when they combined into Headway, now known as Methodist Evangelicals Together. He preached up and down the country – and how fitting that the very last service at which he preached was in the small rural chapel within the Chipping Norton Circuit where his father had started his ministry in 1945, and just four miles from where his mother was born and is buried.

Brian Hoare writes: 'Rob was never at ease with structures and systems, and had a somewhat love-hate relationship with official Methodism. He was always loyal to it, but reserved the right to be critical when he deemed it necessary, yet always with the objective of helping to bring the denomination back to its evangelical roots when he felt it had lost its way.'

Colin Rowe comments: 'In my time working with Rob I always felt he was humbly glad to be one of John Wesley's preachers.'

Paul Smith writes: 'He was a Methodist in the Wesleyan tradition. The "Four Alls" were at the centre of his heart. Like Wesley, he had nothing to do but to save souls. He loved the church when it enabled this to happen, but grew very frustrated when it constrained his evangelistic drive.'

Bob Kitching reflects: 'My personal opinion of Rob was that he was a convinced Wesleyan in his preaching and theology. In fact some would say an evangelical Methodist of the old school. He had an innovative evangelistic Wesleyan approach but could be highly critical of the Methodist system.'

Those comments from people working with Rob sum up the tension of his relationship with his church very well, but as Brian Hoare says: 'I believe that the current recognition of evangelism as being one of the core tasks of the Methodist Church is due in no small measure to Rob's work and ministry over many years.'

Rob's memorial service was held in my church, Methodist Central Hall Westminster, the so-called 'Cathedral of Methodism'. About 2,300 people turned up to pay tribute to Rob, the vast majority of them Methodists. It was fitting that the service was in a Central Hall. His early experience of the life of those great Methodist Central Halls where his father had ministered meant that Rob was returning to his roots. But who else could have filled that great Hall but Rob, one of Mr Wesley's preachers, whose ability to pack a venue continued even in death!

Rob as a Pioneering Visionary

Emma Morrice

When I sat down and tried to think about who I would describe as a pioneering visionary, I came up with John Wimber, Charles Wesley, William Carey – and, of course, Jesus himself (though he was in a league all of his own!). Before I ever became involved with anything Rob-related, I would have imagined a pioneering visionary as someone tall, with a loud voice, who is good at striding across rooms and mountains. Someone very wise and slightly aloof, who thinks long and hard before dispensing a pearl of wisdom to the gathered masses. Someone who does not think of food and other practical, earthly things but is busy being serious. Probably someone whom I would not totally understand, while totally agreeing with them at the same time. Someone who has a core inner strength and is holy in an untouchable way. Their support team would be punctual, suited and booted, very organized and slightly scary in an always-two-steps-ahead way.

Well, I have known the Share Jesus team for nine years now and I've worked there for long enough to know that that's a fairly accurate description of them, minus the odd boot here and there.

However, since Rob was short, he scampered rather than strode (although he tried to stride), and he thought that walking up Haytor on Dartmoor was an extreme hike. Aloof was something he could never be, and his pearls of wisdom, although numerous, normally had an unconventional three or four points to them.

Food was something he took very seriously, especially food of the cooked-breakfast variety. Rob was down to earth but had a thought process that was hard to keep up with, follow or predict. If anyone were to come up with a crazy idea, Rob would take it one step further, so jesting about certain things could prove dangerous!

The idea of filming the second series of *The Frost Debate* (a TV show for the God Channel) at Easter People was put forward as a joke, in that the five-day schedule was just too complicated as it was, starting at dawn and finishing well into the night, with an office team stretched to the limits, and only about five weeks to go. Adding three hours of filming to all that could never have been meant seriously. However, a giggling Rob refused to see that this was logistically impossible and concluded that he was halving my workload, as most of the guests for the TV show were in Blackpool for Easter People anyway, so it would be easy to find them. He did admit afterwards that it might have been 'a little ambitious'. But it worked.

So how did Rob come to shatter my stereotypes and redefine my understanding of the term 'pioneer'? The dictionary definition of a pioneer is as follows:

A *pioneer* . . . is a person or entity that is one of the first to do something. A pioneer may settle previously uninhabited territory, or open up new areas of thought or research. The word is derived from the French language (French: *pionnier*), from Old French peonier, foot soldier, from the root *peon*, in turn derived from *pedn*, from Late Latin, 'one who has broad feet'. . . .

The notions of walking and construction also apply to the American English use of 'pioneer' to refer to a settler, a person who has migrated to a less occupied area and established permanent residence there, often to colonize the area. In this usage, pioneers are usually among the first to an area, whereas settlers can arrive after first settlement and join others. . . . Another common use is to establish one as an innovator in a particular field, i.e.: 'Mr Smith is a pioneer in the teaching profession. . . .'

(*Wikipedia*)

I can certainly testify to the fact that Rob was consistently ahead of the game, accurately predicting future trends in thought and behaviour. He had a reputation for his cutting-edge initiatives, and our projects reflected this. He was never afraid to be the first person to do something.

A pioneer is also defined in some dictionaries as an animal or plant species that establishes itself in a previously barren environment. Rob could talk to anyone and often did. He would quite often return with tales of unlikely encounters with strangers he had met on the train or plane or just in the street. He prayed with a lot of people, and often he took unsuspecting folk, who might otherwise have settled for an easy life, out of their comfort zone and had them building God's Kingdom in a new Share Jesus project, or talking with other visionaries on his radio show. I believe that this simple relational style of life, with a reliance on God, is one that a lot of people strive for and yet complicate. Rob had a principle of, 'If it's getting too complicated, walk away.' He very rarely ended up walking away, as he could simplify most situations and partnerships in an enviable way.

But what made him a visionary? A visionary is defined as:

> one who experiences a vision or apparition. A vision can be polit-
> ical, religious, environmental, social, or technological in nature.
>
> By extension, visionary came to mean also a person with a clear,
> distinctive and specific (in some details) vision of the future, usu-
> ally connected with advances in technology or political arrange-
> ments. Other visionaries simply imagine what does not yet exist
> (but might be as visioning provides a glimpse of the future). . . .
> Some visionaries emphasize communication, and some assume a
> figurehead role, rather than a practical implementation of visions.
>
> (*Wikipedia*)

Well, we can safely remove the detail related to technology (images of a very concentrated Rob, index fingers poised, rapidly jabbing the life out of a computer keypad, come to mind). Rob excelled at the visioning and communication that must precede practical implementation. He was an amazing communicator on numerous levels. He was fortunate in not being bound by practicalities, and thus his visioning knew no limits.

A large part of Rob's ministry was enabling others, developing their gifts and giving them a platform on which to try something out. When someone on his team thought that God had put something on their heart, Rob would give them £500 and let them get on with it. Projects such as 'Thirst for Life' were developed like this. Being given the support and freedom to make and shape a national campaign which challenged thousands of people was an amazing experience. Rob would always have time for us if we needed to talk about something, but he was never possessive of an idea or concept. He was spontaneous and open-minded. 'Thinking outside of the box' would be a good phrase to use, only it would have been hard to keep Rob still for long enough to get him into a box!

The making of *The Frost Debate* was, for Rob, the fulfilment of a lifetime's dream. He had always been fascinated by the media. He never let go of this dream, and eventually he was able to develop this ministry in a very successful way. The Frost Debate was a twelve-programme TV series looking at moral and ethical issues. The aim was to explore the character of God and to encourage Christians to wrestle with and develop their own ideas on topics such as medical ethics, climate change, famine and aid, discrimination, and multi-culturalism. In a matter of weeks we did what a mainstream production crew would have spent months working on – writing scripts and booking up a very high-profile list of guests.

The arts centre (formerly a church) next door to the Share Jesus office was perfect as a film set. It also had the enormous power supply that a five-camera unit would need. A set designer happened to pop into the office with some time on his hands and a few brilliant ideas. Looking back, what we achieved would have been impossible without an incredible amount of blessing. If we had worried about the practical details – such as no budget, no studio and a lack of experience – we would never have got started. But by stepping out in faith and trusting in God rather than leaning on our own understanding, we ended up producing one of the God Channel's most popular and widely viewed series.

This pilot series led to two additional series in quick succession, and we were planning the fourth until a few days before Rob died. He found out he had cancer the day after the filming for the third series had finished.

Hope for Planet Earth, a tour addressing the Christian response to climate change, was another concept that Rob helped to pioneer. The tour has gone ahead and is proving to be incredibly successful and well received. This was yet another first in its field, with other organizations wishing they had thought about it and wanting to be involved.

Rob died with a full diary of engagements and lots of dreams. He often finished his talks, programmes and conversations with an encouragement and a challenge. I feel that this passage in Acts not only sums up Rob's life in many ways but also provides a challenge to all of us, which is exactly what Rob would have wanted:

> So when they met together, they asked him, 'Lord, are you at this time going to restore the kingdom to Israel?'
>
> He said to them: 'It is not for you to know the times or dates the Father has set by his own authority. But you will receive power when the Holy Spirit comes on you; and you will be my witnesses in Jerusalem, and in all Judea and Samaria, and to the ends of the earth.'
>
> After he said this, he was taken up before their very eyes, and a cloud hid him from their sight.
>
> They were looking intently up into the sky as he was going, when suddenly two men dressed in white stood beside them. 'Men of Galilee,' they said, 'why do you stand here looking into the sky? This same Jesus, who has been taken from you into heaven, will come back in the same way you have seen him go into heaven.'
>
> (Acts 1:6–11)

I think this passage encourages us to focus not on heaven but on the mission clearly laid out in Matthew 28:19–20. The passage in Acts firstly talks about the Kingdom of God, and my understanding is that the disciples were wondering about an earthly kingdom, free from the relentless oppression of the

Romans. Jesus speaks firstly about a spiritual Kingdom where we are empowered by the Holy Spirit.

Rob lived his life in a spiritual way, seeking God's will and purpose with the aim of furthering his Kingdom. The power of the Holy Spirit does not limit. He gives boldness, courage, confidence, insight, authority and ability. Knowing Rob, I think these were all qualities that he possessed. His soul belonged to God and his life's actions were dedicated 100 per cent to him. Rob sought to live his life in God's strength, not his own, and had little pride or arrogance. He would kneel with anyone, anywhere, never being concerned with how this might look.

The disciples in this passage were looking at the sky, where Jesus had gone. Now if I had been there, I think I would possibly have done the same. I would have been looking up, thinking, 'Wow! That's great! Oh, how I want to go there with him!'

However, two men dressed in white appear and basically say, 'What are you doing looking to the heavens? Focus on the mission!'

We Christians can get caught up in looking to heaven. It's important to have a heavenwards perspective, but we need to balance this with getting on with what Jesus has commissioned us to do – that is, to spread the word of God to all nations. Rob was totally focused on telling people about the love of God and the importance of a relationship with him, and I think his final three points would have been:

1. Seek God and then get on with it.
2. Don't be bound by practicalities.
3. Keep happy.

Rob as a Preacher

Matt Bird,
Director, Make It Happen

A purposeful preacher

The Big Top crowd hushed as the speaker launched into his opening story. They had no idea where he was going but they knew this small guy would have a big point to make. Just as the story hooked the audience, a young man sprang forward from the front row and leapt onto the platform. The stewards were caught out as the intruder reached the preacher before they could react and defuse the situation. To the shock of the crowd, the young man took a swipe at the speaker, who managed to duck out of the way just in time. Then the speaker delivered a left jab and a right hook, and the young man hit the floor. The crowd gasped. The speaker stood victorious and, just to ensure compliance from this young upstart, he aimed a solid kick into the gut of his victim, who lay groaning and virtually motionless.

The speaker was the Revd Dr Rob Frost and the young man was me. Rob reached out an arm to help me up as he introduced his theme for the evening – 'The daily battle between good and evil that faces us all'. Rob and I had spent all afternoon practising our fight routine to the point where it looked utterly convincing. We had even briefed the stewards to expect a little action, as I was concerned that one of them might turn out to be the Karate Kid and take me out before we could explain!

Rob Frost was a great communicator, a prolific author, a broadcast enthusiast, a media opportunist, a political lobbyist and, most of all, a unique preacher who would go to great lengths to make his point.

Methodism has often encouraged its preachers, lay and ordained, to 'tell them what you are going to tell them', then 'tell them', and then 'tell them what you have told them'. In the Wesley tradition, Rob preached the Bible and encouraged everyone to apply the message in their own lives as well as in the communities in which they lived. Listening to Rob never left you in any doubt about what his point was – it was pushed home to you again, again and again.

Rob stood out as a preacher because he always spoke with a very clear purpose. He preached to motivate people into action, to impart sound biblical teaching and to give a rational explanation of the Christian faith; but most of all, his focus was on inviting people to relinquish their lives to Jesus Christ.

The author of the book of Ecclesiastes states: 'Of making many books there is no end, and much study wearies the body.' Having been a Christian for twenty years, read many books and listened to numerous sermons, it is clear to me that Christianity remains something simple to understand but so difficult to carry out. It can be summed up in one word: 'relinquishment'. Christianity isn't a decision. Although it starts there, it is a lifestyle of surrender to Jesus Christ. It is not a static fact but a dynamic reality that we wrestle with every minute of each day. It is life lived in total and utter relinquishment to the God of the universe – our life wrapped up in the life and pleasures of God. As Henri Nouwen says in his book *Reaching Out*: 'A man or woman who has developed solitude of the heart is no longer pulled apart by the most divergent stimuli of the surrounding world but is able to perceive and understand this world from a quiet inner centre.'

Rob loved his God. He found and nurtured this inner centre through times of prayer while walking on Wimbledon Common close to his home, and wherever he could carve out time to be with his God.

A tireless preacher

Unannounced, a long-haired clergyman from another era walked across the hall, his coat-tails sweeping behind him. He stopped in a central position and began to speak. The audience was American and they listened with delight as the man spoke in a clear English accent:

> On Wednesday 24th May 1738. . . . In the evening I went unwillingly to a society in Aldersgate Street, where one was reading Luther's preface to the Epistle to the Romans. About a quarter before nine, while he was describing the change which God works in the heart through faith in Christ, I felt my heart strangely warmed. I felt I did trust in Christ, Christ alone for salvation; and an assurance was given me that He had taken away my sins, even mine, and saved me from the law of sin and death.

The crowd was silent and still, captivated by what they had heard. The clergyman slowly left the room and another man stood and began to address the crowd:

> The Revd John Wesley began a renewal movement within the Church of England. He invited people inside and outside the Church to a radical commitment to Jesus Christ. He preached on horseback, he preached in the open air and he preached whenever he had the opportunity. He encouraged believers to meet in small groups to spur one another on in following Jesus Christ. . . .

This was another Frost performance, supported by the young Matt Bird (who, incidentally, hates dressing up, especially with a wig – even as John Wesley!).

John Wesley was tireless in preaching the gospel and mobilizing a movement of others to do the same. Whilst Rob Frost and John Wesley were very different men, they shared this characteristic.

Rob had a remarkable energy and seized every opportunity he could to preach. He could engage children at a kids' club, teaching them a fun song before talking to them about Jesus. He took part in theological debates with great intellect and insight in order to persuade others about Jesus. He graciously preached to those who were not necessarily his advocates, and won them over to himself and therefore to Christ by his humility. The projects that Rob developed through his ministry mobilized tens of thousands to make God known in new, fresh and innovative ways: such as young people like me, who took part in one of his Seed Teams, planting new churches; or ministers leading short-term missions; or volunteers taking part in the Easter People festival. One of his strategies for reaching new people was to ask his hosts to put together a choir or a drama or dance group, knowing that their friends and family members would come to see them and perhaps hear about Jesus Christ for the first time. Rob had the knack of creating opportunities for people to both hear about God and serve Him.

A pastoral preacher

A teenage boy nervously arrived at the meeting point for a summer project. What he saw confirmed some of his worst fears about 'keen' Christians – arm-waving, pretending to speak in their 'special' language, and general over-enthusiasm. Christians they may be, but 'freaks' seemed a better description.

There was, however, a consolation for this young lad, as he began to regret his hasty decision to join this summer project. He noticed a couple of girls of his own age; they were Jesus freaks, but it looked as though there could be something normal about them. The three soon became friends and, being young and full of life, got up to all sorts of antics. Whilst relatively innocent, they were perceived by others on the team, and particularly by the leaders, as troublesome and rebellious.

In fact, the more the leaders of the team confronted the trio's behaviour, particularly the young lad's, the less notice they took and the more they played up. The team leaders naturally talked to the Director of the summer project and discussed the possibility of taking the teenage boy off the team or even sending him home. The Director insisted that the teenager should be given as many chances as it took. At the end of the project the boy surrendered his life to Jesus Christ.

As a teenager, that was the start of my journey as a follower of Jesus. It was also the start of my friendship with the Director of that summer project – Rob Frost.

Rob combined his preaching to the masses with an incredible capacity for one-to-one relationships as a discipler and pastor. As a mentor Rob believed in those he was mentoring more than they believed in themselves. He believed in me when I felt out of my depth, he believed in me when I felt nervous, and he believed in me when I had failed, and he did this for many others. He created opportunities for people to serve, and coaxed them into stepping beyond their comfort zones to try something new, all the time pointing people to Jesus. When someone was having a tough time, I remember Rob talking about the 'Christian plod', encouraging people to 'keep on keeping on', taking small steps to keep on going.

Despite his demanding schedule, he also had a wonderful pastoral ministry to so many people. A family within our local community in Wimbledon experienced the tragic death of their son, and Rob was the first to be at their side. A young lady whose romance ended had her surrogate father Rob as a shoulder to cry on. When my own career took a turn for the worse, Rob was there offering his unconditional love and support – even a flat and a job! There are so many people for whom Rob was there at critical moments in their lives. Rob was a special pastor and comforter in time of pain and anguish to countless people.

The ability he had, not only to preach God's love powerfully, but to show God's love to the people around him, was something that authenticated his ministry above anything else.

An unwinding preacher

In a very humble dwelling in the former Soviet country of Estonia, a group of people gathered for a meal. Prior to dinner, the host offered his male guests the opportunity to experience a traditional home sauna. The gentlemen followed their host into what looked like a shed attached to the back of the house, and there the host stripped naked. The guests were a little more timid than their host but followed suit. They were then led into a small sauna where they began to relax. Their bodies were comforted by the unusual ferocity of the dry heat. After ten minutes the host invited the guests to stand and to bend over the bench on which they sat. Some laddish comments and worried looks were exchanged. The host then took what looked like some branches from a bush out of a bucket and began beating each man from the nape of his neck to his ankles. As he did so, he yelped with delight! The guests were then asked to turn around so that they could be beaten similarly on the front. Frost and Bird were among the guests experiencing this special local hospitality after leading a mission in the town.

Rob thrived on having a good laugh after having a good preach. After a preaching gig, he loved sharing a funny story or two over a late-night curry. He was always willing to tell a story against himself, such as his embarrassment at the time of the sauna experience. Radio interviews with Rob were always followed by the offer of a coffee or a greasy-spoon breakfast, and a laugh was always guaranteed. He thrived on hanging out with people, having fun with his mates.

The voice of a preacher

On a summer team-mission from Bible College, the Principal was listening to one of his students preach on the streets. To the disappointment of the student, the Principal wandered off into the town centre, perhaps to get some supplies. When the student finished the Principal reappeared. The student mentioned that he had not heard him out, only to be told, 'I could hear you clearly six streets away!' This was a conversation between Howard Belbin and the young student Rob Frost.

Rob always spoke about his faith in Jesus Christ with fervour and passion. If he needed to, he could project his voice like few others. On occasions he preached so much, with such energy, that his voice would become hoarse and almost disappear, but Rob just kept on preaching.

Rob had a knack for preaching to all manner of people, in a way that resembles the preaching ministry of the Wesley brothers centuries before. He always faced up to the issues of the day. Opening a subject, developing it and applying it were prominent aspects of Rob's delivery. Whether he spoke softly or loudly, you always got it. He was a master in using the right delivery method for each audience he addressed. Audiences and congregations alike were left in no doubt as to his central message.

An urgent preacher

A group of Bible college students leading a short-term mission in a local church took time during the week to hang out with and befriend a group of local teenagers, who consequently attended a special finale event that the students were hosting. During the evening someone preached about Jesus Christ and invited the teenagers to become Christians. Some of the teenagers responded positively and surrendered their lives to Jesus. That night one of them was tragically killed in a fatal motorbike accident.

Rob was one of the students, and the experience confirmed to him that he should spend his career preaching the gospel of Jesus Christ. He would often tell this story to underline the sense of urgency about responding to Jesus.

Thinking about urgency brings some well-known phrases to mind: 'Don't put off till tomorrow what you can do today' (a common saying); 'Today is the day of salvation' (2 Cor. 6:2); and 'Drink your best wine today because you don't know what tomorrow will hold' (yours truly).

Billy Graham is acclaimed worldwide as one of the greatest preachers of the last century. People who hear Billy preach for the first time sometimes comment about how ordinary his preaching is. What is extraordinary is the response to God that Billy invokes in people. Something similar could be said of Rob – that he was a great preacher because God used him and his sense of urgency as an evangelist to draw people to Jesus.

A humble preacher

At a large Christian festival where Rob was speaking, he was asked, 'What would you like to achieve in your lifetime?' My mind began to race with thoughts of what grand schemes he might utter – the renewal of Methodism, the conversion of millions, or global evangelization. Instead Rob responded, 'I would like to have served faithfully.' What a humble aspiration – and he most certainly fulfilled it.

I first met Rob Frost in 1988. I was already a regular churchgoer, but as a result of his ministry, I responded to the invitation to surrender my life to Jesus Christ. Over the twenty years that followed Rob became my friend, mentor and father figure. I thank God for Rob, the communicator who helped thousands of people, just like me, to give their lives to Jesus Christ. He is God's man.

Rob as an Author

Charlotte Hubback,
Editor, Authentic Media

Honest, brave, passionate: these are the words that spring to mind when I think of Rob.

This honesty was a hallmark of his book *Destiny*. It was one of the first that I worked on at Authentic Media and I was much taken with the characters of Ron, Rob, Andy and Chris as they came across on the page. Andy and Chris were a similar age to me and reminded me of my brother and I, subject to the pressures of our generation. Rob seemed a true child of the sixties – questioning, ardent and impatient with unnecessary tradition. His willingness to make himself vulnerable made this book special. This vulnerability was one of the best aspects of his character, and something that informed many of his books. In *Destiny* he was candid about how he felt he had failed as a father at times (and also about his deep gratitude for his eventual reconciliation with both of his sons).

Rob was also unafraid to share his experiences of professional failure: the time when officialdom turned down his plans for a mission centre in the heart of London is a moving example. He was candid about his frustration with Soul Survivor when their plans overlapped with Share Jesus International's. But it was admirable that he was able to be this open, as he could then go on to recount his meeting with Mike Pilivachi and the eventual (excellent) outcome. He was able to show clearly how failure is a springboard to turn us back to God: and encouraging others to do this was something of which he never tired.

This lack of pride applied to his faith as well. He held fast to his core evangelical Christian beliefs, but he was adept at drawing from an eclectic range of traditions to inform his faith and spirituality. He refused to think in a narrow way and would, for example, use the customs of Celtic Christianity to feed his devotional time with God. Rob was open to new ideas and bodies of thought, and he fully engaged with the world. I was particularly impressed by his links with the political sphere. When he supplied his list for possible commenders for his book *Freedom Fighters: Defending Christian Freedoms in a Politically Correct Age*, it was packed full of the names of those who walk our corridors of power. Too often we remain shut up in our churches, only concerned with looking after those inside. Rob knew that this attitude was not enough.

The first I heard of *Freedom Fighters* was a phone call from Rob in the autumn of 2006. He was worried about forthcoming legislation that would possibly restrict Christians' freedom to tell the gospel, and, in typical Rob style, he was actively campaigning against it and doing all he could to inform the body of the church of what was happening. The book looked at the issue of Christian freedom in the UK from different perspectives, and Rob solicited contributions from a wide range of thinkers including Don Horrocks, Nick Spencer and Ram Gidoomal. Prior to this, these people had all appeared on his radio show. His guests there were always drawn from varied walks of life and demonstrated the breadth of his interests.

Despite his many eminent connections, Rob never seemed to have trouble retaining his humility. His book, *Five Things I Wish They'd Told Me When I Became a Christian* is a brilliant example of this. He wrote over twenty books, but I must admit to a completely biased opinion that this is the best. It covers big issues such as discipleship, suffering and discerning God's call, with a deep wisdom informing the writing throughout. He was always willing to admit that he still had much to learn, and his readiness to listen and respond to others was a great strength.

Humility might not be the first quality that springs to mind when you think of Rob: I suspect it's more likely you would think of him as an innovative visionary. One only has to look at the sheer range of projects that SJI was involved with over the years to see that this is true. Rob believed that vision with action could change the world, and he never hesitated to apply this belief. He writes in *Five Things* that no one ever encouraged him to dream a dream, create a strategy and roll up his sleeves – but I'm not sure how much encouragement he needed. Dreaming and planning seemed to come naturally to him. I remember having lunch with him last spring: he outlined seven book ideas and we then tried to choose between them. Some authors would kill to be that creative!

His creativity with books was echoed in his projects. After the decision to bring Easter People to an end had been made, the SJI team went through a thorough process to decide what should follow it. To aid their decision-making, they gathered together Christians from different arenas – publishing, the music business, charities and churches. That day the team enabled us all to do some blue-sky thinking, and Rob was at the centre of it – he was a great facilitator. His and Andy's determination to find the right project eventually resulted in the vision for Pentecost 08, which promises to be a massive weekend party with hundreds of free events across London. SJI envisage a multi-cultural celebration filling hundreds of venues from coffee-shops to pubs to boats. I don't think anyone else would have been quite brave enough to take on something of such complexity, but the team worked out a logical structure, and as I write, I know that all the plans are coming together.

This determination also came to the fore during the production of Rob's books. Writing was one of his key gifts and he took a keen interest in all aspects of production – with a particular focus on the cover. Design fascinated him. I roughed out the cover for *Five Things* according to his dictation, on his mobile phone from a conference. He was horribly busy but made time to return my urgent calls. The result was a striking and effective cover that no doubt helped sales. Publishers quite often wish that authors would leave us to get on with the cover on our own and not be quite so keen on their own idea, but this example shows that we should at times banish that attitude.

Rob's determination and vision were matched by his bravery. On one occasion he was told that he could only preach if he was in possession of a form signed in triplicate by regional and national members of a denomination. This restriction was not imposed on any other minister in the country. We can only imagine how devastating that must have been for him. But he picked himself up and carried on.

I hope Rob is not coming across as some sort of paragon, as one of the qualities that endeared him to me was his sheer 'human-ness'. He loved gossip (Ros, a member of the SJI staff whose husband worked in Buckingham Palace, used to share titbits of Royal news with Rob, which he much enjoyed!) and came across as being very, very normal. When we met together he would love to talk about his latest books and projects, but our chat would always eventually become more light-hearted – a particular highlight being the time when he confessed he was on the Atkins diet in order to fit into his tails for Chris's wedding. When hearing other people's memories of him recently, I was amused by the frequent references to take-aways – fish and chips, McDonald's and Chinese food were mentioned a lot. I suspect these may explain the need for the Atkins diet!

This normality helped him connect with a wide range of people. The thing that touched me, above all, about Rob was the fact that he listened to me and connected with me. I felt valued when with him. Over 2,000 people came to his memorial service, and time and time again, I seemed to hear a similar thing from the contributors. His ability to connect with people was an exceptional gift.

One man at the service spoke of how Rob invited him to be the team pastor at Easter People, primarily to give him a place. I realized then that Rob did the same for me. By speaking to me as an equal, despite my youth, inviting me on his radio show and trusting me with the production of his books, he made my place in the world of Christian publishing just a little bit more secure.

Perhaps he was able to bless others like this because he had been so richly blessed himself. Loving parents, a supportive wife and two caring and passionate sons were blessings he never took for granted. He would always acknowledge that it was only through God's grace and love that he had done more than he ever thought possible.

Rob was more at home in the creative arena than the administrative, and he was careful to acknowledge the help of Marian, Linn, Camille and latterly Emma. Camille was in her late twenties and was unfailingly warm and friendly. Her diagnosis of cancer marked a new stage in my understanding of Rob. He had an almost fatherly concern for his sweet PA and would always be up on her latest treatment and prognosis. He galvanized me and the Authentic staff to prayer and we felt particularly close to the Share Jesus staff at this time. It was good to be able to send Camille flowers and books and receive gracious emails from Rob in return. Despite the many prayers, Camille passed away less than a year after her diagnosis. Her faith and selflessness inspired Rob and led him to a new understanding of suffering.

I remember the day we heard of Rob's cancer. Strangely, it did not cross my mind that he would die: his prayers would be passionate and surely the love of his family and many hundreds of supporters would overcome this battle.

I still find it hard to believe he's actually gone. I half expect the phone to ring and it will be him on the line, excitedly recounting a book idea, or outlining an event he'd love Authentic to be part of. I want to go out to lunch with him and confide my theological struggles, career issues or moral dilemmas – as well as swapping the latest gossip. When I heard about his death, I wept.

If Rob could read this piece now, I'm sure he wouldn't approve of this much praise: he wouldn't want words wasted on him but would urge me to talk of Jesus.

So this is the challenge I leave with you today. Rob was a worthy servant of God and his life inspires me to live more wholeheartedly for Christ. What did his life mean to you and does it do the same for you?

Part 2

Rob Frost in Private

Rob as a Boss

Marian Izzard,
Deputy Director, Share Jesus International

As the longest-serving member of Rob's office team, I guess I must be the person who knew him best in a working capacity. It was never my intention to work with Rob for a twenty-year stint, I can tell you! I started working with him back in 1987 for a period of 'six months to a year' on the Breaking Bread project, with a view to finding 'a proper job' after that.

The ensuing years opened up other opportunities – such as becoming the co-ordinator of Easter People and managing the tours, including Gospel End, Pilgrims, Jubilate and Hopes & Dreams, as well as smaller projects such as walking expeditions and holiday events.

Working with Rob has been not only an amazing privilege, but an incredible journey of creativity, hard work, fun and adventure! At times it was like a rollercoaster ride, as we experienced the thrill of seeing vision becoming a reality and saw exciting new projects birthed and come to fruition. Yet we also rode the waves of disappointment and despair when difficult issues arose, such as lack of finance or circumstances beyond our control, when we seemed to lurch from one crisis to another.

However, Rob was always an optimist and had the amazing capacity to 'keep the show on the road', despite the ups and downs, and was determined to see a way through a problem or issue with some radical idea or proposal which was often quite ingenious and enterprising.

Rob was a visionary, an entrepreneur, a risk-taker and a shrewd businessman. He would have done well as a corporate chief executive, earning a fortune, and jokingly he used to remark on this from time to time. But he knew his calling and loved his work, and rejoiced in his freedom to be who he was, specializing in his many giftings.

As a visionary, he had a constant flow of ideas for new projects or books and dreams for the future. It was quite amazing and often mind-blowing to work alongside someone with this kind of brain! It was refreshing, on the one hand, with a constant breeze of new challenges and options, which kept us all alert and on our toes; but it was irritating, on the other hand, as this kind of gifting sees the bigger picture and the end product, but not always how to get there! This brought with it some frustrations, such as the moving of goal-posts and the changing of plans.

Many a day he would arrive at the office saying, 'I woke up in the middle of the night and had another idea about that programme we were working on yesterday.' I would inwardly groan and would look at him with a pained, fixed expression on my face, dreading what he would say about this new vision and change of plan.

He would often approach the subject by saying, 'You probably won't agree to this, but I shall say it anyway . . .' I knew then that we were in for a big shift in all the work which had been done the day before, and which I had spent my evening finishing off! I have to admit that often this resulted in a greatly improved programme – but I would have preferred less hassle!

As an entrepreneur, Rob delighted in the creativity, action and buzz of setting up new initiatives and projects, but once they were up and running, he was very happy to move on to something else, having 'been there and done that'.

Rob was by nature a risk-taker and enjoyed the excitement and thrill of living on the edge – which was exciting for him, but it pushed many of us beyond our comfort zones. Really this was good for us, but sometimes it happened when we didn't want it or need it!

Being a shrewd businessman, Rob was always keen to drive a hard bargain – always trying to get something for nothing and someone to do something for nothing, whether it was finding a good deal on accommodation or rail fares, or getting a professional band to take part in Easter People.

No matter how long and hard we researched, negotiated or pushed to get a rock-bottom price, Rob was seldom satisfied – he believed he could secure a better deal. And he nearly always could, which was hugely frustrating! In the end we let him do all his bookings, which he was more than happy to do, because he knew he was better at it than anyone else!

Rob was also a futurist – he spent a lot of his time thinking, dreaming and scheming about the future. He was always on to the next thing and would never stand still! Even just two days into a new tour on the road, he would be quizzing me about what I thought we should be doing for a tour the following year! This would always catch me out, as I was just about coping with the complexities of the present project and trying to sort out the finer details, whether it was the bookstall resources for that evening, or where we were going to bank the money, or rearranging the transport for the team for the next day.

Even though Rob drove me to distraction a lot of the time, we had a great working relationship because we were so different. In fact we complemented each other. He had the big vision and the ideas; I concentrated on making these visions become realities, by trying to put some practicality into them. Some of Rob's ideas were so bizarre and mad-cap that I was stretched to the limit to make them work!

Rob hated admin and working on details. It was all very boring to him. He could never actually see admin. He was often described by one of our team as knowing where B was from A, but not always knowing the process of getting from A to B.

Rob was a hard taskmaster and often had the unrealistic expectation that everyone worked at the same pace as he. He would pile the work on. The more one would accomplish, the more he would give, not realizing that it would sap the energy of the poor colleague, who would inevitably 'go under' with a huge workload. He would then be very apologetic and become very pastoral, suggesting that they should take the next couple of days off (but, strangely, expecting the work still to get done!).

Rob was certainly an action man. He had the drive and desire to make things happen and didn't waste time in the process! You knew that if you gave Rob a situation or a problem, he would do his very best to resolve it with you.

He was also a 'man of the moment'. More often than not, he wanted things done *Now*, saying, 'This is really urgent! It's come to the top of the pile' – expecting everyone to jump to their feet and deliver there and then, totally oblivious to any pressure that he might be exerting on people.

He would reel off a whole lot of jobs to be done – emails to be sent, press releases to write, phone calls to be made, strategies to sort. Then he would decide that he had brain-ache, go for a thirty-minute lunch break, and expect it all to be done when he got back, and then wonder what the problem was when it wasn't!

Having been re-energized and recharged by his '2 for 1 Big Breakfast', he would be ready to roll again with some more ideas and another flow of work, as well as deciding to reshape and reschedule what he had decided earlier that morning. He would be unaware that his poor colleagues would need to get some sustenance in them and de-stress before they could continue! Often, it was just as well that no action had been taken whilst he was out at lunch, as he would come back and change it all anyway!

We never quite knew whether it was better with Rob in the office or out, as in the office he was like a whirlwind, but out of it, whether at home or away, you could guarantee that he would phone up about eight times per morning as he moved from one issue to another. Trying to get work done was pretty impossible!

We had an 'early warning system' so that we knew when Rob was about to come into the office. This enabled us to clear the decks, save the programmes we were working on and complete our emails, because once he had arrived, chaos ensued! And that was the morning or the afternoon gone.

When in full flow, he would have three or four of us running around in circles after him as he leap-frogged from one subject to another and 'emptied his brain' of things to do, actions to take, phone calls to make. He would do an amazing multi-task effort all at the same time, dictating letters, making phone calls – sometimes concurrently, with one ear to his mobile and the other to the landline, getting someone to line up a conference call to happen in the next ten minutes involving about ten people to brainstorm the next project. Meanwhile he would pull out file after file, looking for various papers and documents he wanted, and then he would decide that he needed to look at all the Easter People photos for the past eighteen years and see them spread out on a table so that he could select what he was looking for!

He would then look up things on the web, book air fares for the next six trips, proof the next prayer-letter, interact with the youth team, have a laugh, make a joke, sit with his feet on the desk and drink his weak, black tea, which he would never finish.

Because he was often determined to get things sorted and *Now*, he had the annoying habit of asking several people to do the same job at the same time. If he was out of the office he would often phone up three of us, one after the other, and explain the task, whether it was booking flights to the Channel Isles, phoning up a load of MPs for his next TV series, or doing some research for his next book.

From his perspective, this was to ensure that the job got done, and his philosophy was that the more people he asked, the more certainty there was that it would be done, and done quickly! So then, half-way through a job, we would find out that there were several people on the same case. It didn't go down well at all!

He wasn't at all supportive of anyone going on a health and safety course, because he thought they were a waste of time and money. He flagrantly disregarded health and safety issues in the office, littering the entire floor with boxes, sermon files, bags, coats and piles of paperwork, blocking access and doorways and causing visitors and delivery men to tiptoe and trip up. Sometimes it was like working with a cross between a mad professor and Mr Bean!

Rob knew how to work hard and play hard. He was always up for others to join him in his 'down time', whether that was a visit to the movies, pizza in his lounge with a video/DVD, or a 2 for 1 special meal deal at Weatherspoons. He never drank, although if he was feeling particularly stressed or wanting to be 'one of the drinking crowd', he would step out and order a Kaliber alcohol-free lager!

He would unwind by re-telling his day, often with grossly exaggerated stories recounting conversations and situations. He always tried to find the amusing side of things, often convulsing into guffaws of raucous laughter. He would find these times with members of the office team hugely therapeutic in 'getting his blood pressure down' – often as he chomped his way through a huge burger and chips or an apple pie, delighting in his cholesterol intake as it recharged and re-energized him and made him feel a whole lot better. The only slimming effort he made was to drink Diet Coke!

When he went away on holiday, it was a sigh of relief. But the way he recharged his batteries was to draft his next book, or plan the next tour, or dream up ideas for the next project. He would then return re-energized(!), with piles of work and action-plans.

Rob was always grateful for all that was done by all of us in the office – from volunteers and part-timers to full-time, long-suffering staff – and he would take time to say that he appreciated our hard work. He often said that he was a rotten boss and a hard taskmaster who expected the impossible. This may have been true at times, but we wouldn't have wanted him any different. He was a great boss, a man of great esteem, unique, and a privilege to work alongside. He enjoyed being a friend as well as a boss and was very caring towards his colleagues, ensuring that each was valued, appreciated and affirmed.

A truly amazing guy. I wouldn't have missed working with him for the world!

Rob as a Friend

David Heron,
Chairman, Premier Radio and Trustee, Share Jesus International

Rob's memorial service on Saturday, 12 January 2008 truly was a celebration of his life. At Central Hall Westminster, the people in the 2,000-strong congregation were asked from the platform to raise their hand if they felt that they had a special friendship with Rob. I looked round to see who else felt as I did – there was a sea of hands! I wasn't the only one, as I had supposed. Just thinking about this incident makes me smile. Rob was a friend to so many people.

Initially, our friendship grew through time spent together at Premier Radio. Rob was one of the original team of broadcasters at its launch in 1995. I met him when I joined Premier a few months later. We hit it off and over subsequent years became very good friends. I wish I had met him earlier. Knowing him has meant more than I can say.

So, inevitably, one of my lasting memories of Rob is of him in our studios, behind a mike, newspapers everywhere, a clutch of guests exploring issues of the day. Rob was passionate about bringing faith to bear on current issues and making people think them through. Disconcertingly, perhaps as an aid to concentration, Rob would often have his eyes closed as he interviewed someone! I occasionally reviewed the papers on Rob's programme. I would prepare some good stories to share, but he never asked me about the things I had prepared!

Rob was a friend not only to me at Premier. His pastoral heart reached out to many others also. His gift of sensing people's pain or suffering meant that he was in Premier talking to staff and to listeners after many of the great tragedies in recent years: Princess Diana's death, 9/11, the 7/7 bombings in London, and the Boxing Day Tsunami spring instantly to mind.

Rob didn't let down his wider group of Premier friends either. A planned Premier pilgrimage to Israel, to be led by Rob, unravelled with many cancellations after the bombs started falling back in 2000. Instead of the anticipated 5,000 people, the pilgrimage eventually had just 250 bookings. Rob of course fulfilled his commitments and led a most worthwhile and memorable event.

For some years, I have been a trustee of Share Jesus International. This showed me a different side to Rob – he was still the same visionary, he still had the same evangelist's heart, but I saw the wheeling and dealing side of Rob, as he made sure all of us did exactly what he needed us to do!

Rob and I had meals together from time to time. Latterly, the café overlooking the concourse at Waterloo Station worked well for both of us. Some mornings, Rob would arrange to see a whole series of people and would spend three to four hours there. It was a bit like having an audience at the Palace, as we waited for one meeting to finish so ours could begin!

It was there that I first understood how ill Rob was. Getting him to admit it rather than brush off enquiries about his health with the customary 'fine' was very hard at first. I was distressed to hear about the great pain he had been suffering and the loss of mobility in his arm, but clearly, it was even more difficult for him to talk about it. He had always hated talking about himself.

In the end our friendship was suddenly terminated by his death. It is ironic that someone who spent his life exploring life's difficult issues should, by dying so suddenly – and, to our eyes, tragically – make me and many other friends seek an answer to the obvious question: 'God, why?'

Truthfully, both Rob and I found it easier to talk about the media than about ourselves. Maybe that's a 'man thing'. I don't think either of us found it easy to talk about personal issues or problems. Rob's involvement with TV was very important to him and I fully appreciated the risk he was running by appearing on Christian TV, as his historic supporters were not really great watchers of these channels.

We explored going on holiday together, but the dates didn't quite fit. Our wives met up – I wonder what they said about us!

Rob led a ridiculously busy life. We often accused each other of being workaholics! In spite of that, Rob always had time to talk and to pray. It seemed that he had a different number of hours in his days!

Last Easter, 2007, I was at home in the New Forest, recovering from surgery. One friend trekked down from London to see me – guess who?! He came down straight after his Sunday morning show.

So my personal experience of Rob was utterly consistent with his public persona – a highly intelligent and inquisitive presenter with the compassionate heart of a pastor. There were two exceptions. In person, he was extraordinarily modest and self-deprecating, which is not always the case with internationally known speakers. Also, it was clear in public how hectic his life was, but in private, his busyness always gave way to a friend's call. In spite of an incredibly busy life, he always had time to talk and to pray with his friends. That was why so many hands were raised at Central Hall that day.

The verse of Scripture that has been on my mind since my friend's death is Acts 13:36, which is a tribute to King David. Luke writes: 'For David served the purpose of God in his own generation.' How true that was of Rob's life also.

Rob as a Son

Revd Ronald William Frost

Robert William Frost (not to be confused with Robert Frost, the famous American poet) had the misfortune to be born into a Methodist Manse. This meant that when he was three years old, he had to leave the small town in Yorkshire where he was born, and go to live in Stoke on Trent. When just old enough to move from Primary School to Junior School, he had to go and live in Plymouth. Having won a scholarship to Plymouth College, he had to transfer to Birmingham High School, where he was embarrassed to find that the curriculum was entirely different. He did all this without complaint, although it always meant breaking happy friendships.

His mother, who was his most intimate confidante, must, I think, have counselled him to good behaviour – for I certainly didn't! I think she was concerned that his taking part in school-boy pranks would damage my public image as the minister of a large city-centre church.

Joining the Sea Scouts while he was in Plymouth helped him to adopt a high moral code. Although sometimes he gave us anxiety because he joined in adventurous exploits, we knew that he always prepared for them carefully, and that his undoubted courage was matched with practice and knowledge.

As a young teenager while we lived in Plymouth, he was not satisfied until, like the other boys, he could swim out to the Breakwater and back. Then he learnt to handle many different kinds of sea-going craft, and was considered so adept at sailing that he was selected, with only nine other boys, to handle a traditional three-masted schooner.

In addition to keeping the vessel afloat, they had to do their own cooking and keep everything 'ship-shape and Bristol fashion'. The exercise was to sail the craft across the English Channel and along the canals of Belgium and Holland. Then they had to take it out onto the North Sea and stay out of sight of land for three days, mooring the boat on Dogger Bank.

You can imagine how relieved we were to see him home safely after three weeks' absence, and how sincere our congratulations were when he received his Scout Badge certifying his achievement.

Only a week or two later, I was most unexpectedly ordered to leave Plymouth to become the Superintendent Minister of the Birmingham Central Hall. There can be few places in Great Britain further from the coast, and I could see that Robert was pining for water.

Consequently, on our first Saturday afternoon in Birmingham, I drove him to Cannon Hill Park, gave him half a crown, and told him to get a rowing-boat out on its large lake. When he had gone, I settled down to put the finishing touches to the next day's sermon.

About fifteen minutes later, however, he returned and he was very upset. The boating-lake attendant had taken one look at his small stature, and assuming him to be younger than his fifteen years, had told him that he could not possibly be responsible enough to hire one of their boats! The problem was soon resolved when I went with him and explained the situation. Once he got established at his new school, he joined their sailing club and his love of water activities never left him.

I have reported that incident because it seems to me to typify the whole of his life. He didn't complain at moving away from his friends. He rarely complained about anything, and had a real genius for friendship. He didn't mind living in a variety of different places. He loved travelling and ultimately preached the gospel in India, China, America, Brazil and a whole host of other places.

Robert's adherence to the Scout Law and Promise matured into a quest for John Wesley's Scriptural Holiness, and with the aid of the Holy Spirit he sought to achieve Christian Perfection.

He appeared to take risks, such as when he smuggled a mini-bus load of New Testaments into Yugoslavia for his college friend Keetan to use. He was, however, never foolhardy, for he always informed himself of the conditions that prevailed, wherever he was going.

It would be wrong to assume that, because Birmingham was far from the sea, he disliked it. Nothing could be further from the truth. It was there that he surrendered his life to Jesus, and felt the call of God to be a preacher of the gospel. Although not much older than the children from poorer families who benefited from the Birmingham Mission's six-week camp that was held each summer, there he displayed the gift for leadership that was to be so valuable in later life.

It was also in Britain's Second City that he first showed his ingenuity in attracting people to gather to hear the gospel. For it was there that he insisted that the terms 'Youth Club' and 'Youth Fellowship' needed updating. 'Call them the Chyps,' he said, meaning the 'Central Hall Young People's Society'. Of course, he was right. City-centre layabouts, University students and young people from church families all enjoyed themselves together, and many who otherwise would have had no contact with the church came under its influence, having 'Chyps with everything!'

This is how I see Robert William Frost, my beloved son. But it must never be forgotten that he was also the son of my dear departed wife, Freda Mary (née Williams). Now they rejoice together in Glory.

Rob as a Husband

Jacqui Frost

**I call upon these persons here present to witness that
I, Jacqui Thornton, do take thee, Robert Frost, to be
my lawful wedded husband . . .**

At the age of 17, my ideal man would have been tall, blond
and athletic . . . and then I met Rob! He was short, weighed
eight stone and wore outdated clothes from charity shops.
While studying for the Methodist ministry in 1972, he was
leading an Easter mission at the church I went to in Moss Side,
Manchester. He drove me home in his battered car at ten miles
an hour, explaining that girls only fancied him because of his
leadership skills. I understood why this would be the case but
didn't say a word. Our first informal date was a trip to the
local park, where he sat on the roundabout while I pushed –
that was, until he asked me to stop because he felt sick!

In the summer Rob went to Kenya for six months, and on
the day he returned I went to Kenya with CMS to work as a
teacher for a year. On the tube in London I told him our relationship was over. Once in Nairobi, I sent him a letter with the
single word 'Sorry' on it. He spent time with numerous theological students trying to work out whether it meant 'Sorry,
but it had to end' or 'Sorry that you are hurt' or 'Sorry, I didn't
mean what I said'. I had meant 'Sorry, but it had to end.'

On my return to Manchester the following year, I found that
Rob had organized a holiday with friends and a September college course for me – I was furious! We went on the holiday but
it was disastrous because I didn't want to be organized. Then

one night Rob said it would be good to pray – what could I say? So we did. I still don't understand it to this day, but I began to fall in love with Rob, and by December we were engaged. By the following June we were married, and by September we were in South Elmsall, Yorkshire, for Rob's probationary year as a minister in charge of three churches.

. . . to have and to hold from this day forward . . .

On one of the first days in South Elmsall, we were both trying to sort out the garden. Some neighbours passed by and told their friends, 'Isn't it wonderful there are teenagers helping out the minister with his garden?'

We were young, and while Rob (aged 25) enthusiastically worked to encourage the churches and their work in the community, I, with no understanding of 'being a minister's wife', was struggling to darn socks and make bread, while taking seriously the advice I'd been given that I should have no friends in the churches, in case of favouritism!

Our three years in Yorkshire were difficult for us, as we worked together on what it meant to 'be married'. Rob did his first weddings, funerals and prison visits, conducted three services most Sundays, and struggled through the *Constitutional Practice and Discipline of the Methodist Church (CPD)* before each church meeting.

We both enjoyed working with young people, and in our holidays we took them on mission trips, telling people about Jesus in East Anglia, Spain and America. Life with Rob was never going to be boring! I loved his gift of living, and in thirty-two years of marriage, I never tired of his conversation and insight. Like his mother, Rob loved telling stories, and he certainly had many amazing experiences to talk about.

. . . for better, for worse . . .

In 1979 we moved to Mitcham. We were both excited at the prospect of living near to London. Andy and Chris were born, and while I enjoyed time with the other mothers and their children in 'the nappy club' (Rob's name for it!), he worked hard initiating new ideas. It was during this time that he felt the calling of God to do freelance work for the Kingdom. So at the end of five years we agreed to leave Methodism, if necessary, to make this possible. Don English came to the rescue with a house in Cheam and a grant from the Rank Trust, and so we had some stability for our family. I remember asking God at this time for financial security – that however much Rob went away, there would always be money in the bank at the end of the quarter. Throughout our marriage God has been faithful in providing in amazing ways!

So Rob started his nomadic life, fulfilling his God-given dreams – and probably some 'not so God-given dreams'. It meant we had to work out our marriage in a new context. Rob would come home buzzing with news, and I had spent my days caring for the children and 'keeping house'. Rob came home expecting to be 'in charge', but I had been the one 'in charge' and managing without him. Nevertheless, it was exciting to hear about God at work and to know that he could use ordinary people to do extraordinary things.

In 1986 I became Rob's third wife! Later he said, half joking, that he had six wives in total: 1. 'the home maker'; 2. 'the mother'; 3. 'the student'; 4. 'the teacher'; 5. 'the LAC director'; and 6. 'the artist'. I felt that it kept the interest alive in our marriage, but he struggled with all of the changes!

I had always assumed that I was not very capable academically, but in 1986 Rob encouraged me to study for a degree in drama – although neither of us had thought through the implications. I was told by a female lecturer that I was an insecure, marginalized wife, and I suppose in some senses she was right. During the course I became more assertive, and Rob and I had to work through this 'more equal' relationship.

He enjoyed his fourth wife, 'the teacher', who was fulfilled and bringing in a good salary. But while Rob had plans for me to become a head teacher, in 1994 I felt God's call to leave teaching and set up the Lantern Arts Centre (LAC), based in Raynes Park Methodist Church – with no three-year plan and no secured salary!

The first five years were really difficult. On the surface things looked great – but where do people in leadership go when life gets tough? During that time, when I felt I was 'running on empty', I was so thankful that I could hang onto the knowledge that it was God who had given me my love for Rob in the first place. I suppose I had often 'hidden behind' Rob, and so we never realized that in fact we had quite similar personalities. Rob never liked to be 'boxed', but when we agreed to do a Myers Briggs personality test, we found out that we both had the same four preferences. Interestingly, you're not supposed to marry someone that similar! But the information helped us both to understand our roles: we weren't in competition, but were moving in parallel lines. So we could enjoy our similarities while looking for others to 'cover our backs'.

. . . for richer, for poorer . . .

Every January Rob wrote a list of targets for himself for the year ahead. There was always a work list, with the books he would like to write, his ideas for the media and plans for Easter People. There was also a 'spiritual to do list', which included personal areas such as prayer and service to others. And there was often a list of physical aims for the year, but these always had words before them like 'try to' or 'attempt to' – and, unlike the work and spiritual aims, few of these were ticked off by the end of the year!

I thank God that we are all made differently and that one-year and three-year plans are not for me! But on New Year's Day 2003 Rob asked me if I had a list and, as I began to talk, I decided that I would like to take up stitching again, which I hadn't done for years. So Rob took the initiative and found the only day course in London, which happened to be on my day off, and enrolled me . . . and I loved it! The only problem was that the course closed, and then I was faced with a choice of no course or working towards a degree . . . so I set off on a degree course. Rob was pleased I was working in textiles on the day course, but he was more troubled when the house began to resemble a studio and the hours involved became excessive. Then he had the shock of finding he had a sixth wife – 'the textile artist'. In floods of tears, I explained that I wanted to stop work at the LAC, do the last year of the degree while supervising those who would take over at the LAC, and become an artist. Poor Rob – with so many projects of his own, he did find it difficult that his wife changed course so often! While he helped me to write the letter of resignation, he wondered how we would manage financially and, more importantly, how we would manage without our circle of friends.

. . . in sickness and in health . . .

I am so glad that I became Rob's 'sixth wife' because, while the work on the degree and the commissions was demanding, I could work my hours alongside his. So for the last year we were able to spend more time together – going places, doing things and simply enjoying being together. When Rob was diagnosed with cancer in June 2007, we both thanked God for his leading, which meant we could do the hospital visits together, drink cappuccinos together and cry together.

While Rob wrote poems and prayers about his struggle with cancer, putting words to that lonely place where he felt very insecure, he continued to share his story with others in need, continued to challenge others to live 'in Christ' and continued to live each day to the full.

During our last week together, in October 2007, Rob said he was sorry for so often giving me the 'ends of his days' when he was exhausted from work and had no energy left. I agreed that that had often been true for me and the boys, but that I wouldn't have wanted anyone else to be my husband. He was exhausted that week and we know now that the cancer was spreading rapidly. We spent three hours on a bench, looking over the sea, and talked and laughed about the 50-mile coastal path walk we had done in August. We had struggled up to Haytor with the wind against us, determined not to give in. We had sat in beach cafes, drinking stewed tea, and quietly reflecting.

Rob loved life and was always positive. On the Wednesday before he died he was working on an MA course for the students of London Bible College. I am really glad that he kept working and always had hope for the future. He wanted, more than anything else, to encourage the next generation, and I'm glad that he didn't hide away with the cancer and give up hope. Even in the last week in Devon, Rob was not sure if he felt ill because of the radiotherapy, or because of the medication, or because of the cancer. Driving back from Devon, he asked me to cancel his appointments for three months so we could assess what was happening, but the next day in the hospital he was feeling much better and only wanted his appointments cancelled for two weeks!

. . . to love and to cherish . . .

Rob always loved the media. He enjoyed watching television and DVDs and going to the cinema, but his real joy came when he was actively involved in radio and television programmes. It was never difficult for Rob to get out of bed at 6.30 a.m. on a Sunday morning to work on Premier Radio and, down the years, he enjoyed being part of a number of television programmes. He was so thankful to the God Channel for the opportunity to do *The Frost Debate* in his last year. In the first years of our marriage a television programmer had considered Rob and I to do a 'double act', but I had never been very keen to be involved. In June 2007, just before we knew Rob had cancer, I agreed to work on his 'arts debate' with him. In this way, I was able to share his television dream in a way that I couldn't when I was in my twenties. I am so glad we were able to work together – and although I have not been able to view the shows yet, they are precious memories. Sharing important events together is a brilliant way to keep love alive.

Rob enjoyed celebrations, and Christmas was a time for family and friends – the more the better! Despite all of Rob's commitments and travels, we had wonderful holidays as a family, with friends, and just the two of us alone.

. . . till death us do part . . .

In our culture and in the church we don't talk enough about death. Rob and I loved life, but we often discussed death over the years. We had not planned a funeral or worked out practical details, but we talked about one of us living without the other and the reality of the 'new heaven and earth'.

Rob was always there for people in a crisis. While he struggled as a minister with routine pastoral visiting, he was brilliant at finding the time to visit people when they were ill, going through a crisis or recently bereaved. He would listen, without judgment, as they talked about their real struggles, and then he would pray or even inject a little humour – whatever seemed right at the time.

Rob loved his Premier Radio show and meeting with the guests for breakfast afterwards. But because of the show, and other engagements, he didn't always manage to get to church on a Sunday, which was a sadness to him. He did, however, get the opportunity to visit lots of different churches and denominations. In the final months he enjoyed early morning communion in the Anglican Church – just the quietness and reflective atmosphere.

On the Sunday before he died he was up and dressed by 7.30 a.m., but for the first time said that he felt sick and went back to bed. I knew this was serious. He slept late but still managed a full roast dinner – although sleeping for seconds at a time with a fork of food halfway to his mouth.

One of my prayers for Rob was that he would never lose his appetite, because he loved his 'rubbish' food. Six days before he died he ate an 'English breakfast in a bap' and was delighted because the shop gave him a reduced rate – Rob loved a bargain to the end! Even in hospital, he was enjoying the food and on the Friday I fed him tinned peaches, which he really enjoyed. (I remembered feeding my dad rice pudding just before he died and hoped this would not be Rob's last meal).

While eating the peaches (which in fact turned out to be Rob's last meal), he was talking to us as a family and encouraging us to go out and enjoy the weekend. He was also telling the nurses how wonderful we all were and telling us how fantastic the nurses were! On the Friday night, as they tried for the third time to get a line in his neck, he was encouraging the doctor to try again! Although they were giving him a litre of water an hour, he was still very thirsty. Rob had preached on the Easter story many times in the months before his death. It was therefore poignant for me that he had his 'Good Friday' of pain and thirst when, for the first time, things seemed bleak to him and he thought he would die. On the Saturday he was medicated and, although we talked to him, we're not sure how much he heard. On the Sunday he was resurrected to life eternal!

When the medication was gradually lessened on the Sunday, Rob became more alert but couldn't speak because of the ventilator. Andy, Chris and I had our 'seven special minutes' with him on that day.

We told him, through our tears, how much we loved him . . . that it was time for him to 'let go' . . . that it would not be long before he would be with his heavenly Father . . . that we would all be sad, but we'd be all right.

Rob tried to speak and Andy said we understood that he wanted to tell us that he loved us . . . and he smiled with his mouth and eyes.

He was also conscious when his father, Ron, visited. He sang his own verse of 'All for Jesus', dedicated to Rob.

After other precious moments with friends and family, Rob died peacefully at 11.40 p.m.

. . . according to God's holy law . . .

When Rob left the Easter People stage for the last time in March 2007, he was thinking how sad that it would be the last Easter People after twenty years. But he heard God's voice speaking to his mind and saying he wouldn't be here next year. When recounting this to me in June, just after the diagnosis of the cancer, I knew it was a word from God. While Rob still hoped for five years, I merely hoped we would have a family Christmas together. I am sad that we didn't, and I don't understand God's timings, but I realize that all my mourning is for me and not for Rob. He is in a place of greater reality and greater love.

In the last week Rob kept repeating that he did not want to live in pain and unable to be active. I do believe, however painful this is for me, that it was God's grace that brought about such a sudden end. Neither of us would have coped well with prolonged illness, and that is simply a reality. The prognosis of his cancer was not good and to have seen him slowly and painfully 'disappear' would, I believe, have been beyond both of us. I do not understand how other people manage and I have the greatest respect for all those who suffer and care. I also trust that God knows us intimately and will give us the strength to go through the situations that are within our capabilities and will not expect more. I have to remember this as I now face being a single adult for the first time in my life!

Probably there are always regrets when someone dies – the conversation not had, the problem left unresolved, the kiss not given. While Rob really wanted to live and was ever hopeful for more years, he always said that dying or living was a 'win/win' situation for him – to live with me or to live with Christ. But he recognized that for me it would be a 'win/lose' situation because I would miss him so much. Death is such a 'wrong thing' and I believe it was never part of God's plan. The story of Lazarus has helped me, because I see in it the 'totally human' Jesus experiencing the death of one of his best friends, and crying . . .

. . . and to this I pledge myself . . .

Rob and I had enjoyed our flat in Bovey Tracey for six years – it was a place where we could escape and have time together. In the summer of 2006 we bought a house, and I remember standing in the garden and asking the Lord why we had this house now, long before retirement. I said that I hoped it was not because Rob was going to die and I was going to live there alone, because that was not what I wanted. I also acknowledged that if this was to happen, then I would see it as the Lord's providence.

How strange now to stand in the same spot in the garden –
alone. This is not what I wanted, and yet it is God's provision,
for which I thank him.

As Rob would have wished, I will 'live my life', but . . .

I will miss you, Rob.

Rob as a Dad

Chris Frost

I have been avoiding writing these words for some time, as contemplating memories of my Dad changes the weather of my emotions, blowing the dark clouds of grief overhead.

I had told my Dad to write an autobiography for some time. . . . If only he'd listened, he'd have saved me a job! But I think that for him, to write an autobiography would have been waving a white flag to the cancer and admitting death was imminent. That was something he was never willing to do.

He was always a fighter – not the type you would see in the scenes of a Hollywood epic by any means, but one who would fill you with faith and courage. I remember when I failed to get on the university course I wanted to be on and didn't have a clue what to do with my life. Dad, instead of admitting defeat and offering sympathetic words, encouraged me to ask the course tutor (okay, he dialled the number and passed me the phone!) for a position considering my experience – and he gave me one!

This fighting spirit was epitomized through Dad's classic catchphrase: 'We've gotta keep on keeping on!' He was superb at helping people see outside their situations and at encouraging them not to give up. It was this dogged perseverance that never failed to win my respect. I will never forget the time we went to preach at a retreat for a church in Singapore. He got pretty sick out there, catching some sort of virus. He lay in bed one evening, groaning and mumbling, barely able to walk to the toilet. I said I'd let the leaders know that he wouldn't be able to preach that evening, but he was having none of it. Sure enough, just a couple of hours and some ibuprofen later, he was on the platform, calling people to submit to Christ. Later he collapsed in a heap in the hotel room.

Having a Dad who spent a lot of time on the platform did come with its struggles. There were times when he would have to be away from the home for prolonged periods. And I hated being introduced to people as 'Rob Frost's son' rather than Chris. Part of the struggle was that, whilst everyone knew my Dad as the great evangelist, author and church leader, to me he was first and foremost my Dad. He was the guy who would stand at the touch-line of my football matches and cheer me on, no matter how badly I played; the one who would watch *Big Breakfast* with me before school, or take me for a greasy fry-up on a Saturday morning.

Dad would often say: 'I just want to be your mate, Chris.' I remember when I told him of my frustration that I couldn't have a beer with him like my mates could with their dads because he was a teetotaller. Always willing to help, he started taking me and Andy to the pub, ordering two half pints of lager for us (very uncool!) and a bottle of non-alcoholic beer for himself (also very uncool!).

Looking back, I can honestly say he was one of my closest friends. We could spend hours chatting to each other about everything and nothing. We loved discussing films, theology, ethics and broadcasting – we really sparked off each other in conversation.

He loved to tell me his funny stories. He had a brilliant way of building interest in them by starting with, 'Have I not told you this yet? I can't believe you haven't heard it!'

One of my most important memories of my Dad is of him on his death-bed. We all have moments in our life which, at the time, just pass without our noticing, yet with hindsight turn out to be extremely significant; this was one of them. It was late one evening, just a couple of days before he died, and one of the last times I heard him speak. He called Andy and I close to him, held our hands and told us how proud he was of us and how much he loved us. He implored us to take care of Mum. He went on to pray, 'Lord, pass on any anointing I have to these two boys and use them to break the gates of hell and bring many into your Kingdom.' Above all, I will aspire to have the same passion for the Lord and the lost as he always did.

Rob's love for us as a family was incredibly strong and constant, and he has left a legacy of memories in our hearts. These memories, although painful now, are our family's inheritance, passed down so that we may invest similar memories into others.

Like every great man who is no longer with us, it's easy to paint an unobtainable image of greatness – a man who didn't have struggles and weaknesses and who was immune to making the mistakes that the rest of us make. That wasn't my Dad. But it was his 'realness', married to his supernatural care and love, which really made for the best Dad I could ever have hoped for.

Thanks, Dad. You will be greatly missed. Until we meet again.

Part 3

Tributes to Rob Frost

A Tribute to Rob

Bob Kitching,
Methodist minister and Share Jesus International Trustee

What a privilege it was to be a friend of Rob's. I first met him in June 1971 when we candidated for the Methodist ministry. In September we both found ourselves at Hartley Victoria College and became firm friends. I used to say he met Jacqui in the back of my car! What a joy it was to preach at their wedding on 28 June 1975.

Friendship with Rob was never dull. He had a wonderful engaging way of including you in the most bizarre, even madcap schemes, which quite often you agreed to support because of Rob's enthusiasm, sometimes against your better judgement. Rob had a zany, quirky sense of humour. An outing with Rob easily became a jaunt because he would suddenly say, 'Let's go off and visit old Bill Jones!'

He could convince you that his opinion was almost infallible. I remember being on holiday with Rob, Jacqui and the boys and my family in France. Rob spotted in a local paper that there was to be a carnival in a nearby village followed by a *son et lumiere*. Rob convinced us all that in this part of France carnivals were immense and that because it was a bank holiday, we should set off early in order to get parked and purchase tickets for the *son et lumiere*.

We fell in with Rob's plans and, after some grumbling from the more leisurely members of the party, set out. When we finally found the village where the carnival was to take place, there were literally six cars parked in a huge field and some sparse amusements. But Rob, always the enthusiast, said, 'But there's always the *son et lumiere*!' However, when we viewed the set-up, it seemed to consist of a couple of spotlights and a dozen ordinary lightbulbs. Rob found it very funny and so did the rest of us.

Rob was a kind man and would put himself out for his friends. In 1978, when my Mum died, he and Jacqui invited Val and myself, with our one-year-old, to stay with them. When I was in hospital in 1984 and again in 2006, Rob was one of the first visitors I had.

He and Jacqui formed a wonderful hospitable partnership. Who can ever forget spending Christmas with them? We used to travel up from Hampshire saying, 'We wonder who will be there this year!'

I remember going up to the door of 138 Lambton Road and Rob saying, 'Thank goodness you have come! Look after the Koreans.'

'What are their names?' my wife asked.

'I don't know – we only met them this morning.'

Another year Luiz and Elsa Montanheiro's friends from Brazil were there, and so it seemed quite natural that I could ask Rob the next year if we could bring our friend Vanlalsiama from Burma.

On Christmas Day Rob loved to play games – the old favourites like 'Charades' and 'Murder in the Dark'. On Boxing Day he would organize a Wimbledon Common football match.

When you serve in the Methodist ministry, some friendships come naturally to an end because of distance. Rob made a nonsense of distance – he and Jacqui made the effort to keep in touch. Wherever our family have lived – Tipton in the Midlands, Lancashire, Hampshire, Leeds and Devon – Rob and Jacqui and family have always been such wonderful guests. Not only that, but we were made so welcome in their homes. Rob was always interested in you, in your family and in so many other families too. He would go out of his way to share, to help and to pray with you.

Dr Leslie Weatherhead said of his friendship with W.E. Sangster: 'It was all give on his part and all take on mine.' In many ways that is what I feel about Rob's friendship with me. He was a burning and shining light within Methodism and the evangelical world, yet he was my old mate Rob who I met in 1971. For me, he was 'the friend who sticks closer than a brother' (Prov. 18:24).

A Eulogy to Rob

Steve Deal,
Script-writer

It is an honour to be given this opportunity to talk about my friend Rob Frost. Many people have stories to tell about this extraordinary man. Things happened around him and because of him. He was the catalyst for many funny, moving and often life-changing events. It was almost as if his life was one long anecdote. If it was, then I am proud that I had a small part in the story that was Rob Frost's life.

In 1986 he employed my Theatre Company to perform at a Tell It With Joy event in Telford. On the way home we stopped at a café and Rob told us that he had hired a holiday camp on the south coast.

'What – the whole camp?!' I asked.

'Yes,' he replied with a grin, and then a little more quietly, 'I hope people come.'

And that was Rob for you. Whereas you or I might have hired a bed-and-breakfast in Bognor to see how things went, Rob hired an entire Pontin's holiday camp with no guarantee of filling it, other than it was what he felt God wanted him to do.

As it turned out, within a couple of years there wasn't a holiday camp in the country big enough to hold Easter People. What did Rob do? He took over whole towns.

Not all of his ideas came to fruition. At one time he considered hiring a circus big top, but was put off the idea when he learned that he'd also have to hire a team of Hungarian acrobats to put the tent up and down.

I once asked him what he was most proud of, and without hesitation he replied, 'Jacqui and the boys.' When I spoke to him at Easter People 2007, he was almost bursting with pride as he told me about Chris and Jo's wedding and the role Andy was playing in Share Jesus International and other organizations. He also told me that as Easter People wound down, he was looking forward to spending time in Devon with Jacqui, and that he intended to take more of a back seat in the future as others stepped up to take responsibility for the running of Share Jesus. I asked him if he was going to retire, and he said, 'No, I'm just going to slow down a little.'

Rob was an incredibly busy man and sometimes not the easiest person to work for. It was not unheard of for him to ring me in the morning with an idea for a sketch he wanted me to write, and then to ring back two hours later wondering why I hadn't emailed over the first draft; in the meantime he had written two books and organized a pilgrimage to Jerusalem. He would forget that not all of us had his superhuman drive and he would often leave in his wake a trail of people scrabbling to keep up.

When I was desperately ill and lying in intensive care, unable to even breathe without the aid of a machine, I would often wake to find Rob sitting beside my bed. Indeed, on several occasions he sat up all night with my wife Polly just quietly lending support. He fully recognized and accepted that sometimes things would not be all right in the end and that sometimes there are worse things than dying.

Rob loved a bargain and getting a good deal. So much so that our mutual friend Paul Field called him the Arthur Daly of the Christian world. During the Jubilate tour, which took place outdoors and in typical British weather, he managed to get hold of a job lot of umbrellas at a bargain price. He was delighted. I'll never forget the sight of the ladies of the Methodist Guild sheltering underneath umbrellas emblazoned with the logos of Benson and Hedges and a well-known contraceptive brand.

Rob Frost lived the fullest life of anyone I have ever known. He travelled the world sharing his faith in Jesus and headed up an ever-growing organization dedicated to that purpose.

He never flinched from doing what he believed God wanted
him to do. And yet that same, incredibly busy man would happily sit with me drinking coffee and putting the world to
rights. He didn't see the wheelchair, he saw what I was able to
do and he helped me and countless others live a life that
pushed us forward in the service of God.

Rob, if anyone ever deserved to rest in peace, it's you.

Memories of Rob

Roger Forster,
Leader of the Ichthus network of churches

Rob was a visionary – but more than a visionary. He not only saw possibilities and dreamed great dreams, but implemented them in true leadership style – he engaged in them himself!

He worked out the 'How to do it' as well as the 'What to do'. He did this with great zeal and enthusiasm which captured our hearts and persuaded us to follow. Sometimes his schemes seemed 'crack-brained', but this hardly mattered, since generally they worked well and were Christ-honouring. And if they didn't work, there were so many more to come that in no time at all, the failures were lost, forgotten and swallowed up in the multitude of successes.

It would be impossible to name all of Rob's visions – they are too numerous to recall – but they covered radio, television, music, drama, prayer, debates, dance, match-making, journalism, conventions, training and evangelistic tours. You name it, and you would find that Rob had seen some way of utilizing it for the gospel. It was all great fun to participate in with him. We will all miss this practical prophet, or 'seer', as the Bible calls such visionaries.

Rob was not just a God-man or a Spirit-man; he was also a Jesus-man. He loved all he could see of Jesus and wanted to see more.

What visions now fill his view?

Memories of Rob

Gerald Coates,
Leader of the Pioneer network of churches

'Why is it that all the charming, genuine and uncomplicated have died?' someone once asked after a friend's funeral. I'm told there is a headstone somewhere in the USA that reads: 'He never was charming until the day he died.' Of course, it's only right and proper that we remember the good, honourable and charming things about someone when family and friends are grieving over their loss.

However, in Rob Frost's case, it's just about all you can say of him. He was the genuine, gracious, hard-working and charming man we all knew. I was privileged to speak at Easter People and saw what he and his team had achieved, and more recently, I did three radio broadcasts with him.

I have been privileged to support his son Andy in his ministry – something that Rob was not only unthreatened by, but encouraged me to pursue.

He was a pioneer, and unusually creative for a man of his age. He surrounded himself with younger, fresher minds, and it showed in so much that he did.

When I got the call from my office to say that Rob had died, in disbelief I shouted down the phone '*What*?!'

I was totally unprepared. This was because of the dignity and style with which Rob carried himself.

Rob made you feel you were his friend. And, of course, we all were – more, perhaps, than he ever imagined.

A Letter to Rob

Adrian Plass,
Writer

Dear Rob,
You're in heaven now, so I can be as rude as I like. Before I ever met you, I saw a photograph of your face in a magazine. It wasn't a very good likeness and I can remember thinking that you looked like a demented squirrel. Later I came to realize that this wasn't so far off the mark.

You and Jesus and the average demented squirrel always did have one main feature in common: the expenditure of enormous energy and passion in the quest to save as many nuts as possible.

You were a Jesus nut, weren't you, Rob? Whether you were elated or in despair, exhausted or refreshed, encouraged or disappointed, you never lost the desire to see people waking up to the fact that Jesus is whatever light is needed in every conceivable kind of darkness.

My memories of you are like snapshots.

I remember being on stage when you were speaking. You'd asked me to have a few bits and pieces ready so that you could have little breaks when you ran out of steam. After the second of these preaching stretches, you turned away from the microphone and walked towards me at the back of the stage, your face pallid and strained from the sheer passion of communication, your eyes almost crossed with exhaustion.

'Go and do something,' you gasped. 'I'm all preached out . . .'

I remember travelling to do a performance for Lantern Arts, and learning when I arrived that my wife, Bridget, had been involved in a serious accident on the motorway on her way to join me. The love and practical concern that you and Jacqui offered on that nerve-jangling evening is something that I shall never forget.

And I remember sitting on the stage at Easter People in a little semi-circle of people who were going to contribute during the week. You asked us to explain, one by one, why we had come. One person said that he was there because he wanted to see Jesus lifted up and worshipped. Another talked about how he hoped to see the Kingdom increased. The third expressed an aim to see Almighty God glorified. And so it went on. It was all very impressive. I was last. There wasn't much left for me to say, really. All the good stuff had been pinched.

'And why are you here, Adrian?' you asked.

'For the money,' I replied.

You pretended to be shocked.

'I sincerely hope not!' you exclaimed. 'I'll have to see Marian afterwards. We must be paying you too much.'

But you weren't paying us too much, Rob. You weren't paying us too little either, but that wasn't the point. None of us ever did things for you because of the money. We did them because you had one of the greatest gifts of all – the ability to show people that you truly valued them.

Lots of snapshots there. Mini-memories of faces lighting up as you greeted individuals as though that man or woman was the most important person in the world. And you know something, Rob? That was what made things like Easter People so very special. Because that attitude trickled down and affected every aspect of the festival. There were never any second-class Christians at Easter People. What an achievement!

So now you've gone pioneering off to find out if all the stuff we talk about is true. You and I were always going to spend more time together, weren't we, Rob? An evening or two in one of those cosy Sussex pubs that I was always telling you about. It'll have to wait now, but on the new earth the beer will be even better, surely.

I'd better let you go now. You're probably in the middle of persuading Gabriel to take charge of car-parking at some massive divine event.

Thanks for all you were, Rob. I'll miss you.
Cheers, mate.

Watch the Sky Tonight

Paul Field,
Singer-songwriter

watch the sky tonight
there will be stars
there are always stars
sometimes hidden
by clouds, illusion, confusion, darkness

but there are always stars
sometimes one will fall
shoot across the timeless sky
and in an eternal split second burn brighter
and shine
if we glimpse it we are blessed
it will scatter the diamonds of heaven around our feet and guide
    our footsteps
for a few precious seconds of our journey
through clouds, illusion, confusion, darkness

the stars that remain can burn on brighter from its loss
become more radiant through having shared
its power, energy, joy, grace
its beautiful, priceless, irreplaceable verse in the eternal song
there will always be stars
when we glimpse one on its fragile, fleeting journey and touch its light
we have been truly blessed
watch the sky tonight
there will be stars